Illustrated by John Steel

blood banner

PACIFIC PRESS PUBLISHING ASSOCIATION
Mountain View, California   Omaha, Nebraska

To my father,
a lifelong example of loyalty
to his fatherland,
his adopted country,
and his God.

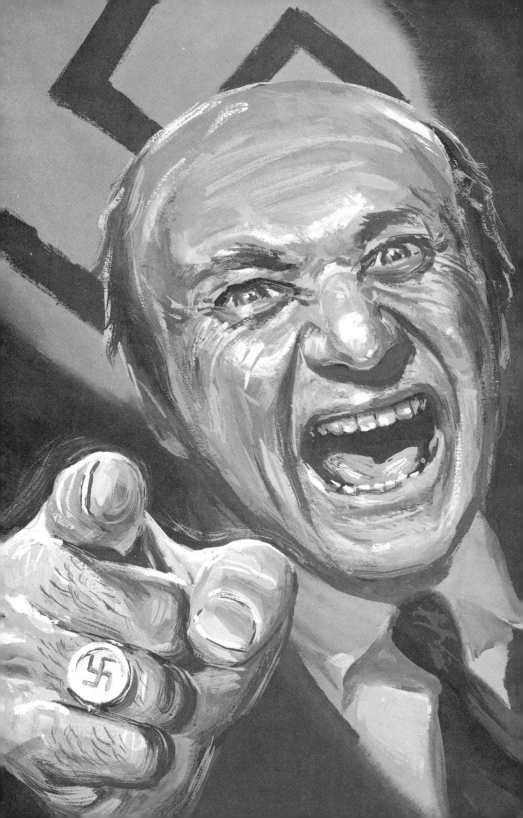

one

HERR MEIER LOOKED over the twenty children at the desks before him. "Eric, you will recite the life story of our *Führer,* Adolf Hitler." He pointed a stubby finger at a fair-haired boy of ten.

"Sir, I do not know the story of Adolf Hitler's life." Eric's voice trembled.

A crimson flush spread over Herr Meier's face and up over his bald head. Anger flashed in his eyes. "You, then, Frevie!" The stabbing finger selected another boy, this one with dark hair and brown eyes. "The story of our *Führer* from childhood to leadership of the German people, and be quick about it!"

"I can't tell it either, sir." Frevie cringed, and Eric could see that his friend's terror exceeded his own.

"Come to the front, both of you." Rage and fear hung in the room like evil odors.

Eric darted a look at Frevie. He knew that his friend felt just as he did. He'd like to dive out that door into the early June springtime and never come back anymore; but neither of them dared. They came forward while the frightened eyes of

"The story of our Führer!" shouted Herr Meier as he pointed a stubby finger at the frightened boy.

their schoolmates followed them and every child in the room sat still. Eric could hear them breathing.

"Bend over!" Herr Meier laid three strokes of his tough bamboo rod on Eric's back—then on Frevie's. The sharp pain and the shame cut Eric with savage force. He did not cry. He looked at Frevie. Both of them were too big to cry, and they had felt the cruel stick before.

Eric didn't know why Frevie hadn't learned about Adolf Hitler's history, but he knew why he himself hadn't. In the Kreye home, Father did not admire Hitler. Eric had heard Father say many times that he wished his boys could have grown up in the United States where he had lived for over ten years.

Eric went back to his desk. His back still smarted from the schoolmaster's rod, and he felt confused. Almost all the German people regarded Adolf Hitler as a great hero. His picture was everywhere—in classrooms, offices, railroad stations, on street corners. A German could scarcely go anywhere without seeing the face of the *Führer* staring down at him. But Father condemned Hitler as a dangerous fanatic. With half of his mind Eric wanted to follow Hitler, but the other half kept telling him that Father could be right.

After school he walked with Frevie and his other friend, Volker, along the country road that led past the big Lutheran church in Holtensen and through lush country meadows and blooming orchards. They swung along under a row of blossoming apple trees following the paved road toward the small village of Unsen. Eric could see his own house standing three stories high. When he got nearer, he could read the sign in front of it, *Hölscher's Gasthaus*. Early flowers—crocuses, tulips, and daffodils—nodded and swayed their bright colors in the front gardens.

The *Gasthaus* (hotel) had room for no more than six guests, but at the front of the house was a small tavern where people came to buy drinks. There was also a large room where four tables seated six guests each. Mother served the best country food, home-baked bread, pies, cakes, and cookies. This same room provided a place for dancing with chairs and tables pushed aside.

The little farm, orchard, and garden provided an abundance of delicious food. The village of Unsen itself lay in a resort area where people came to enjoy vacations in the quiet country atmosphere.

The house and barn were connected by a passageway so that in severe weather no one needed to go outside to do the chores, not even to carry in wood.

Eric felt proud of his home, and he couldn't think of a better place for a boy to live.

He said good-bye to his friends and went around the house to the barns. He found Father and the farmhand, Ludwig, preparing the cows' evening meal.

"Father," he said, "I got another beating at school today."

"And what for this time?" Father looked down at him with a stern face. "I hope you were not discourteous to your teacher."

"I couldn't recite the story of Hitler's life."

Father's blue eyes darkened, and a look of sadness drew sharp lines on his face. He left his work and motioned Eric to follow him outside. Eric knew that Father did not want Ludwig to hear what he intended to say.

"The history of Adolf Hitler can do you no good," Father spoke in whispers. "He is an evil man, and before he has finished with his folly we shall see Germany ruined."

Father looked around with sharp eyes. Eric knew that such talk must not be heard—no, not by anyone. He thought of Frau Schmidt and her one-armed son who lived just across the street. Both of them were rabid Nazis, always looking for some disrespect to the *Führer's* name or position, always listening to catch any word against the *Führer's* plans and to note any person's failure to say, "Heil Hitler."

Eric looked up the back wall of the *Gasthaus* to Frau Hölscher's window. She didn't have it open, so he felt easier. Frau Hölscher's son had leased the *Gasthaus* to the Kreye family, and the fat old woman had been allowed to keep her room on the second floor of the building. Eric knew that she could be mean. She even stole things sometimes. He had no idea what the limits of her meanness might be. He knew Father had good reason for not wanting Frau Hölscher to hear any of his private business, and Father's opinions about Hitler needed to be kept private indeed.

He turned and saw Father looking up at Frau Hölscher's window. Could it be that Father felt the same fear he did. Eric felt a cold fist grab his vital organs and twist them into a knot of anxiety. Ever since Hitler's armies had invaded Poland and war had come to Germany one fear seemed to crowd another.

Father took hold of the boy's shoulder, and for an instant Eric felt the strength and comfort of his father's hand, warm through his light jacket. "If you are ever punished for discourtesy or cheating or other kinds of misbehavior, I will have to punish you myself. But a beating for ignorance of Adolf Hitler's life story is an honor. I am proud of you." Father went back to the barn.

Eric carried his books into the kitchen where Mother was cooking supper on the big stove. "Oh, you are home, Eric!" She turned to smile at him. "How did school go today?"

"As always, Mamma." Eric took a sweet cake from a plate on the table. Then he ran out into the back garden toward the huge pear tree now in full bloom. Wild laughter burst from his throat. He scurried up the trunk of the old tree and swung from one of its higher branches. "Heil Hitler!" he shouted in a mighty voice.

From his high perch he could see the rolling land around Unsen ribboned with the green of new crops—rye, barley, wheat. Fields covered with *Raps* (plants grown for the oily seed) flung deep yellow blankets against the hillsides. He could see where the creek trailed a line of fresh green trees and brush as it curved through the pastures and farmland.

Here in the old pear tree the terrible war seemed far away. He saw only the peaceful beauty of his village home, the bright flowers and orchards heavy with blossom. He tried to shut from his mind the thought of battles and bombed enemy cities and swarms of war planes that Father heard about every night from the radio on the old black piano in the parlor.

Eric knew that a law had been proclaimed forbidding any person to listen to foreign broadcasts. Such listening would be punished as treason. While most of the country people had short-wave bands on their radios, not many of them understood English. In defiance of Hitler's law Father listened to the British Broadcasting Company in London every night.

The news from Berlin blared forth on every street corner and from many shops and private homes. Eric had become so familiar with Hitler's voice that it often wakened him in his dreams at night with some fierce threat. Hitler always used violent words. He always spoke in exaggerated terms. Young as he was, Eric knew that much, and he feared to do anything that might displease the *Führer*.

When Mother called him to supper, he scrambled down from his refuge in the pear tree and went in to take his place between his older brother, Hans, and his little sister, Irmgard.

After supper Hans hurried off to his *Hitler-Jugend* (Hitler

Youth) meeting, and Eric didn't see him again until the older brother crawled into the other bed in the room the boys shared. "What did you do tonight, Hans?"

"We sang songs, listened to stories, drilled and marched with packs on our backs. You know—what we usually do."

"You like it, don't you, Hans? And you like Hitler's plans for a great and powerful Germany?"

"Yes, I like it. Makes me feel like a strong man; makes me feel power; makes me feel how great Germany is."

"I feel that way too sometimes at the *Jungvolk* (Young Folk) meetings," Eric confided. "Do you think I'll make good in the *Hitler-Jugend*? Will I feel the strength more when I get older?"

"Yes, of course." Hans turned his head on his pillow ready for sleep.

"Hans, why doesn't Father feel it too? Why does he object to Hitler's plans?"

Hans' voice sounded muffled and sleepy. "He spent too many years in America. He can't forget what he calls 'the free life' over there."

Long after Hans's deep breathing showed that he slept, Eric lay thinking and listening until the whole village quieted and he could feel how *Hölscher's Gasthaus* lay naked under the sharp stars hiding secrets too dangerous for any house to support.

He fell at last into uneasy sleep where he dreamed of Herr Meier and his mighty bamboo stick; dreamed of running along the open roads and lanes with some frightening thing in pursuit; dreamed of bombs dropping on the roof. He woke to hear Mother calling, "Hans! Eric! Breakfast is ready."

At breakfast Father looked thoughtful. "I'm sure Hitler will make an attack on Russia before long. He is already established in the Scandinavian countries. He has overrun the Balkans and occupied Greece. The Vichy government in France jumps every time Hitler whistles. Russia is his next move." He stabbed a thick slice of bread with his fork. "War is terrible! Great armies go out to kill other armies of men they don't know and can't possibly hate."

Eric ate his pancakes and applesauce while his mind struggled with Father's ideas of war and tried to compare them with Hitler's. All the German youth leaders pictured war as glorious, honorable, and necessary for the future growth and success of the Fatherland. One of Adolf Hitler's sayings darted into Eric's mind:

There will be no peace in Europe until a body is hanging from every lamppost!

He picked up his books and started for school, but he kept thinking about how much Father's ideas differed from Adolf Hitler's and Herr Meier's. He wondered about America. He couldn't remember anything about it because he'd been too young when his parents came back to Germany. One thing he knew, America could not possibly be more beautiful than his home here in Unsen. He looked from the lacy pink apple blossoms along the road to the growing grain fields and beyond to the Süntel (a mountain) where the new green of the beech trees swept up the slopes to meet the dark green of pine forests on the heights.

Eric wondered if other boys felt the same pulse of exquisite pleasure inside—all that color! Those soft green curves and the blue sky tipped like an amethyst bowl overhead.

He reached the corner where his two friends, Frevie and Volker, joined him. "Heil Hitler!" They greeted each other. Every Nazi boy must repeat the greeting many times each day.

The three friends hurried along toward the schoolhouse, but not because they felt eagerness or anticipation for a pleasant day. They carried sharp memories of Herr Meier's stick and his fierce tongue.

"Heil Hitler!" they greeted their teacher. He returned their salutation in full voice, but Eric could see that he seemed to be in no happier mood than yesterday. The boys went to their desks which were sturdy tables placed close together around the room.

Eric felt some unseen, unnamed presence press down on him. The sunny June morning darkened and chilled.

During arithmetic class one boy made a mistake in reciting the multiplication table. He said, "Six times seven is thirty-six."

"Next!" the teacher roared in such a threatening voice that Volker, who was next in line, mumbled, "Six times seven is forty-five."

Herr Meier leaped onto his stout oak desk, crashed several books, rulers, and pencils to the floor, then jumped about on all the desk-tables where the pupils sat. He stamped his heavy booted feet and shook his bamboo rod over the cowering children before him. *"Dummköpfe* [fools]!" he raged. "Why do I waste my time on you?"

Before Herr Meier's fit of anger had cooled, every boy in the arithmetic class had felt the stick, and all the girls were sobbing. None of the boys cried out or showed in any way how much the stick hurt. They had trained in Hitler's *Jungvolk*. Not one of them would admit that he suffered under the teacher's blows or his savage talk.

At home that evening when Eric related the day's happenings, Father looked at him and said, "School is going to be over for this term in just two more weeks. I will try to have you transferred to the *Mittelschule* (middle school) in Hameln before school begins next fall. I'm sure you can pass the entrance examinations."

14

Eric endured the remaining days of school cheered by the thought that next term he would go to a larger school with a bigger playground and more boys. Most of all he hoped that the teachers would not be like Herr Meier.

two

ON A BRIGHT AFTERNOON in late June, 1941, Eric and his two friends, Frevie and Volker, crossed the fields and pastures toward the Süntel where they meant to climb the tower, called the *Süntelturm,* that stood just beyond the mountain's crest. From Unsen they could see the top of the tower rising like a crown into the sky.

The hike usually took an hour, but on this afternoon the boys made it in less time. Startling news had come over the radio in the parlor at home the night before. Father had told the family at breakfast. At school there had been such excitement and rejoicing that the boys could think and talk of nothing else. The German *Wehrmacht* (armies) had crossed the Russian border!

No place, Eric told the other boys, could be so fitting for their own celebration of such news as the *Süntelturm.* They burst in on the restaurant owner who conducted his business on the ground floor of the tower. "Heil Hitler!" they greeted him, and each boy gave him five *Pfennige* (coins) which bought them the right to climb to the tower's upper platform.

"Well, well! I see that the good news has already reached your ears." The man smiled as though he understood just how enthusiastic *Jungvolk* should celebrate such an important event. He opened the door to the spiral staircase, and the boys, following their usual custom, began to run up the stone steps. Perhaps today, spurred by Hitler's advance into Russia, they could run up the one-hundred-eight steps without stopping.

Halfway up and completely out of breath, they paused to rest. Eric noticed how old and worn the steps looked. He wondered how many people had climbed them since the year 1900 when the tower was built. It had stood there ever since pointing its serrated crown to the sky, and everyone knew it as the chief landmark of the area. It could be seen from the valleys on both sides of the Süntel.

The boys came out onto the platform at the top and cried in one breath, "Sieg, Heil! Sieg, Heil!" until the far hills echoed back the ringing shout of victory. Then their impaired breathing forced a moment of silence.

Eric looked down on the lower slope of the mountain toward Unsen and saw Hitler's *Hakenkreuz,* a mighty memorial he had erected to commemorate the rise of the Third Reich. A huge metal swastika set in stone towered above the grassy amphitheater where Nazi meetings and rallies often took place.

Beyond and below lay the whole sunny valley. Beech and pine forests, pastures and meadowland, grainfields, gardens, and orchards stretched across the valley floor. Fruit trees marked the country roads that ran toward Holtensen and Hameln to the south and toward Hannover to the northeast as well as the road that ran from Hasperde to Welliehausen through Unsen and passed in front of his father's *Gasthaus.*

The boys heard the faint chug-chug-chug of a train on the tracks which paralleled the Hannover road. They heard it

17

whistle, and the sound set off another explosion of "Heil Hitler!" from the boys on the tower.

Eric's chest swelled with a wonder he could not explain. The sight of beauty always moved him, and his village home had never looked more enchanting or more peaceful than today.

"Hitler has kept his promise," Volker said, still a little out of breath from the climb and the shouting. "Already this year he has conquered Yugoslavia, Rumania, Bulgaria, and Greece—"

"And now soldiers of the *Wehrmacht* are marching east into Russia." Eric could see in his mind thousands of soldiers advancing in orderly ranks into the huge Russian territory. He could hear their marching song:

> *The rickety bones of the world*
> *Are shivering with fear.*
> *But to us, this fear*
> *Means a great victory.*
> *Today Germany belongs to us—*
> *Tomorrow the whole world!*

"We shall see all Europe a part of the Third Reich. Heil Hitler!" Again and again the boys flung their exultant cries across the wide valleys and against the far hills. Then they sang patriotic songs.

Somehow Eric wished he'd come alone. His friends couldn't be nicer fellows, and he always had fun with them; but today he needed to be alone to wrestle with the great thoughts that struggled up inside him. He gazed out at the calm loveliness of the scene before him and knew for the first time that love for the Fatherland could be a big thing with a boy.

He would grow up to be a man, and he would defend his country with his strong arms and his stout heart. He felt of

18

his arm muscles, hardened through months of training, and wished that he could grow up faster. The *Führer* would have conquered the world before he grew old enough to help.

"Come, we must go." Eric started for the stairway. "We must hurry if we get home before dark."

"Remember, tomorrow is *Jungvolk* meeting," Volker said. "We're going to practice battle maneuvers—sneak attacks and defense." Volker's brown eyes glistened with enthusiasm. "That will be great fun."

"I'm going to be old enough for the *Jungvolk* this autumn." Frevie looked wistfully at the two older boys.

Eric thought Frevie would make a fine *Jungvolk* boy. With his roguish looks, his bright black eyes, and his mischevious face he looked like a little brown elf.

Eric slapped him on the shoulder. "Good, Frevie, we'll be there to clap and shout for you. Heil Hitler!"

The boys did run all the way down the hundred and eight stone steps. After an enthusiastic exchange of greetings with the restaurant owner they hurried home.

Eric left his friends at their turning off points along the way. At the *Gasthaus* he ran into the kitchen where he found Mother putting supper on the table. The thick pea soup and fresh-baked bread smelled so good that he hardly heard Mother's voice. "You are home, Eric. Where have you been since school?"

"Oh, Mother, we climbed the *Süntelturm,* and we shouted and sang for all our victories and for Hitler's ordering our *Wehrmacht* into Russia." He gave his face a few swipes and sat up to the table.

Father had come in now. He washed his hands and looked at Eric with sober sadness in his face, but he said nothing until the whole family sat in their places. Then he spoke in a serious tone. "War is not a happy thing to shout and sing about, Eric. War brings sorrow, pain, and death to many people who have never done us any wrong, and who have as much right to live as we have."

"But, Father, aren't you glad for our *Führer's* victories? Doesn't it make you proud to hear it on the radio?"

Again Eric caught that look of sorrow in Father's eyes. "Nothing about war makes me glad or proud."

Hans looked up, and Eric could see how love for Father and loyalty to Hitler struggled together in his older brother. But Hans said nothing.

The following afternoon when Eric put on his uniform for the *Jungvolk* meeting he thought about Father's words. Why did Father think of war in such a different way? Someone might report Father to the secret police. Then—he dare not think what might happen. He knew that children often reported their parents to the *Gestapo* (secret police). How could a boy do that to his own father?

He drew on the short black trousers and the khaki-colored shirt. He buckled the wide black leather belt with the swastika buckle and arranged his black scarf with great care. He pulled on long socks that reached almost to his knees, and last of all he slipped into his heavy boots.

He looked at himself in the mirror and saw a neat figure— a fair-haired youth with blue eyes and an eager look on his face. Mother always saw to it that his uniform was washed, ironed, and laid out for him on the days when he attended *Jungvolk* meetings. He could always count on Mother. He wondered if she felt as Father did about war.

He started down the stairs and paused for a moment to look at the two old guns that stood in the angle of the stairway. The guns must be very old—muzzle-loaders, both of them. Father had other weapons too, two old swords and a modern rifle. The Kreyes were well supplied with weapons.

20

In the downstairs hall his little sister Irmgard caught his hand. "Oh, Eric, you look so smart and handsome. I wish I could be a boy. I'd make such a good fighter."

Eric laughed and patted her soft braids. "I'm sure you would."

He met Volker on the way to Holtensen, and the two boys marched along together. They held their shoulders straight and behaved with great dignity. They knew that every villager who saw them felt proud of the *Jungvolk*.

This afternoon the *Jungvolk* boys separated into two teams of about twenty-five boys each. The leader of each group carried a compass. Guided by that instrument he led his boys into the forest.

One group concealed themselves in a spot that could be defended. Eric's group were the "attackers." They would try to sneak up on the "enemy" position and take the "defenders" prisoners.

Eric strode along behind his leader keeping his eyes and ears alert for any telltale movement or any slight noise that might reveal the "enemy's" location.

"We are marching north." The leader called all the boys to look at the compass, and he explained how to read directions from it. "Now we will turn east, and I will show you again how the compass works."

As the boys penetrated deeper into the forest, they tried not to make any noise. When they passed through heavily wooded sections, they stepped with care and lifted tree-branches or stepped over dead limbs that might crackle and betray them.

Eric watched for grassy places that might have been trampled and for broken twigs or tracks of any kind.

A short distance after the "attackers" turned east they topped a small knoll. The leader held up his hand in a

21

gesture commanding caution. Along the creek, directly below them, Eric saw something move. He stiffened. The "enemy!"

With stealthy haste the team leader assigned them their "attack" positions. He sent two groups of five boys each to creep up on the "enemy" from behind. They must cross the creek without noise or any awkward movement. Three boys he placed on the left and three more on the right of the "enemy" position. The other boys waited until their teammates were ready. Then they made a frontal attack, leaping forward and shouting, "Sieg, Heil! Sieg, Heil!"

The boys who had been hiding dashed out in a fierce counterattack, but the leaders declared them "prisoners," and then they all laughed and shouted, "Heil Hitler!" They turned toward Holtensen singing the song of the Hitler Youth:

Our flag flutters before us, as into the future
We move man for man.
We are marching for Hitler through night
And through danger,
With the flag of youth for freedom and bread.

Two boys marched in front of each team carrying the swastika flags. Eric thought no flag could be more beautiful than the flag of the Third Reich with its brilliant red background and its white circle with the black *Hakenkreuz* (swastika)—the "blood banner" under which all Hitler's armies marched and fought.

The boys marched through the streets of Holtensen. The villagers stood in their gardens or looked from their windows and waved to the *Jungvolk*. Eric knew that all the other boys must feel just as he did—proud, important, and successful.

They reached the exercise ground at the school, and one of the leaders announced, "At our next meeting we will hold a swimming contest and a discus throwing competition." He

The boys penetrated deeper into the forest. Now along the creek, directly below them, Eric saw something move.

stiffened, and every boy came smartly to attention, his right hand raised. "The Oath! Repeat the Oath of the Sword."

Jungvolk boys are hard, silent, faithful.
Jungvolk boys are comrades.
The highest honor of a Jungvolk boy is honor.
Sieg, Heil! Sieg, Heil! Sieg, Heil!

They dispersed, each to go to his own home.

Eric thought how much he enjoyed the activities of the *Jungvolk:* the hikes, the games, the songs and stories, and the battle exercises like today. He looked forward to the swimming contest and all the other exciting competitions the future offered. He wore the uniform with pride and repeated the Oath of the Sword with fervor. But today had seemed different. Could it be that he had begun to grow up, to know more, to enter into a man's feelings? Today the war-like exercises had stirred new depths in his mind. They had seemed *real!*

With the exciting melody of the song still ringing in his head and the words of the Oath still on his tongue, Eric left his friend, Volker, and turned toward home.

Eric longed for his fourteenth birthday to come so he would be able to join the *Hitler-Jugend.* Hans belonged, and Eric knew that they did a lot of grown-up things, much more serious and important than the *Jungvolk.* He also knew that Hans could hardly wait for his eighteenth birthday when he could enter the *Wehrmacht.* Of course those eighteen-year-olds had to give their first six months to the *Arbeitsdienst* (the work corps). He'd seen pictures of those handsome young soldiers with shovels over their shoulders. He knew they must be an important part of the army. They cleared landing fields, built barracks, dug trenches, and did other necessary work to help and support the fighting men. He'd do that too.

24

Eric's mind jumped ahead, and he saw himself already a uniformed soldier marching with Hitler's *Wehrmacht* toward Stalingrad.

Shouts roused him from his dreamy thoughts, and he saw both Volker and Frevie running to overtake him. "Can't we celebrate some more?" Frevie's dark eyes sparkled with mischief, and Eric knew that Frevie would feel left out until he was old enough to join the *Jungvolk* in the fall.

"Come to my house," Eric suggested. "It'll be a long time until sundown, and I've got a good idea for a celebration."

The three walked along the Holtensen road until they came to the curve that led past the *Gasthaus*. They passed the Rasche farm and the fence that enclosed the *Gasthaus* garden and the hotel itself. Eric led them beyond the big stone-walled barn where they turned off the road and went around behind a brick firehouse that stood near the creek.

Celebration of Hitler's invasion of Russia urged them on to still more exciting demonstrations. The trip to the *Süntelturm* the day before and the exercise of the *Jungvolk* battle maneuvers had not diminished their energy. Eric still bubbled with jubilant emotion.

"Has anyone got a match?" He looked at the other two boys. They began to empty their pockets. Volker found a couple of matches, and Eric explained that a bonfire must be the finest celebration that boys could have.

They scurried around collecting sticks and twigs and small pieces of wood until they had built quite a pile against the back wall of the firehouse.

"Won't the house burn?" Frevie's black eyes sparkled with excitement.

"It's brick. How can brick burn?" Eric replied. And Volker also declared that brick couldn't burn.

Volker scratched a match and held it under a handful of

25

dried grass. Smoke came out, then a small flame. He thrust it among the dry twigs and fire licked up the wall.

The boys danced around their bonfire shouting, "Heil Hitler! Sieg, Heil!" Now and again they scattered to scoop up more fuel for their blaze. A brisk wind sprang up, and the fire became a snapping success. Then the boys saw someone coming.

Eric knew him. They all knew him—the mayor of Unsen! His farm lay just a short distance west. The mayor seemed to have something on his mind. He strode forward and broke into a run. Something in the manner of his coming convinced Eric that he should run too.

He sprinted for the fence and the creek. Every instant he could hear the mayor's heavy feet pounding nearer. He could hear the mayor puffing for breath, and also certain unkind and profane words spouting from the mayor's mouth. Eric ran fast, but he had run and marched and climbed several miles already that day. The mayor's legs must be twice as long as his. In the midst of a wild leap forward, he felt a heavy hand clutch his shoulder. The hand spun him around to face the angry mayor, and then he saw the stout stick in the mayor's hand. He had only an instant to consider its meaning, for the mayor gave him a severe beating.

"Foolish boy!" the man snorted and mopped his forehead. "What mischief will you think of next? With this wind you could have burned the whole village."

Then Eric heard other footsteps more familiar to his ears. "I've put out the fire," Father told the mayor. "I was working in the orchard when I saw the smoke."

Eric saw that Father carried a willow switch. He could never decide, afterward, which hurt the worst, the beating with the mayor's cudgel or the flogging with Father's switch. He wondered about Frevie and Volker. Had they suffered for their celebration? Eric thought it hardly fair that they should be punished for celebrating Hitler's glorious new thrust into Russia.

That night after Mother had come up to hear their prayers and tuck them into bed, he talked to Hans about it.

Hans raised himself up on his elbow. "On my way home I saw Frevie and Volker at Frevie's father's restaurant. They got punished just as you did. I guess you boys better grow up enough not to start fires. We have enough problems without you boys destroying our property with your stupid foolishness."

"But, Hans, the firehouse is brick and—"

"The woodwork inside it isn't brick, and neither are the beams in the roof. I'm disgusted with you. You act like a baby instead of like a *Jungvolk* boy."

No punishment could hurt so much as Hans's scorn. Never again would Eric start any fire near a building. He tried to sleep, but his legs and back felt miserable. He couldn't tell whether he ached from the beatings, the battle exercises today, or the climb up the *Süntelturm* the evening before.

He thought of Father's words at supper the night before. Perhaps war was not so good and glorious. If he felt so distressed from a beating, what must the wounded soldiers feel on the battlefield? What must the people feel whose homes were being burned, looted, and destroyed?

A few days later at breakfast Father said, "Well, Hitler boasts this morning that the greatest battle of annihilation of the war or of all history has taken place east of Kiev."

A few mornings later, in the streets of Holtensen, Eric himself heard the voice of Hitler broadcast over Radio Berlin:

Our forces have dealt Russia a paralyzing blow. We have between five and six million troops in the U.S.S.R.

27

He wondered if Father had heard. He tried to imagine how many five or six million soldiers would be, but his mind failed before the huge figure. His thoughts seemed to reel— Then he remembered the swarms of planes that flew over Unsen every day and probably at night as well. He wondered how many millions of men were fighting in this war on both sides. He felt sick. Would any life survive this madness of destruction?

He hurried home and found Father in the barn. As he so often did, Father hummed a quiet little tune—a cheerful sound—and it always made Eric feel better to hear it. Yes, Father had heard Hitler's broadcast.

"Why does God let them do it?" Eric asked.

"I cannot answer that question. I do not know the mind of God, but I'm sure He doesn't force anyone to do right. We must choose whether we will do right or wrong and take the responsibility for it." Father looked down at Eric and laid his hand on his shoulder. "Cheer up, Son. This war cannot last forever. There are powerful forces on the other side, and they are pushing hard on Hitler's *Wehrmacht*. They will sweep Hitler and his gang of murdering fools to destruction. Wait and see."

"Did you hear something on the radio?"

"Never ask such questions. Just trust my word."

After that day, Eric listened to Hitler's broadcasts with less fear. He knew there were two sides to this war. Father had told him.

three

WHEN SCHOOL OPENED in the autumn of 1941, Eric's father enrolled him in the *Mittelschule* in Hameln. He found Nazi teachers there too, but none so fanatical as Herr Meier.

Eric didn't like being separated from Volker and Frevie. Now he could see them only after school and on weekends. Both Volker and Eric attended the *Jungvolk* meetings in the exercise yard of Eric's old school at Holtensen.

One afternoon the *Jungvolk* meeting held special attraction for Eric and his friends. Frevie would be sworn in as a new member. Eric walked onto the exercise ground and saw the boys forming up into ranks. He hurried to join them. Then he saw Frevie out in front, dressed in his new uniform and looking so proud and important that Eric couldn't help smiling. The youth leader ordered Frevie to stand at attention and salute. "Now, repeat after me the *Jungvolk* oath:"

> *In the presence of this blood banner*
> *Which represents our Führer,*

29

I swear that I will devote all my energies
And my strength to the savior of our country,
   Adolf Hitler.
I am willing and ready
To give up my life for him,
   So help me God.

As the three friends walked home that day, Eric felt as proud of Frevie as he had of himself when he had taken the same oath.

Hitler's advance through Russia had captured the boys' interest and enthusiasm. Hitler even boasted that within six weeks his armies would be in Moscow; but as the autumn days stiffened into winter, Eric began to hear hints that the Russian cold might be severe and the snow deep. The Russian people might prove stubborn too.

One morning in early December Father appeared at the breakfast table looking so grave that Eric felt his heart begin to pound. Mother came to stand at Father's side and laid her hand on his shoulder. "Boys," he began in a husky voice, "the Japanese have made a surprise attack on Pearl Harbor in the Hawaiian Islands and inflicted terrible damage on the United States fleet."

"What does it mean, Father, and why does it worry you?" Eric asked.

"Japan is Germany's ally. Now the United States will declare war on Japan—then on Germany and Italy, and all the nations of the Triple Alliance."

"I'm sure Hitler expected that the United States would come into the war." Hans dished himself another big bowl of applesauce. "He'll know how to take care of those Yanks. Why, the war will be over before they can get started! What's the news from the Russian front this morning?"

Father turned to Hans, and Eric thought he saw a look of

pity in Father's eyes. "My boy, every day of the Russian winter is a hell of agony for our *Wehrmacht*. War is hell!" Father got up without touching his breakfast and went out to the barn.

"Mother, why can't Father see that Hitler knows what he is doing?" Hans looked up with an angry face. "He has pushed ahead to quick success in almost every country in Europe. Remember Dunkirk?"

"Hush, Hans! Your father is a gentle person. He hates war. We lived in the United States for over ten years. If he had been able to choose, he would be there now. He knows much more about America than you do."

Eric had never heard his mother speak so defensively before. He put on his warm coat and mittens, pulled his furlined cap over his ears, and started for school.

In the streets of Holtensen he heard the loud blare of a radio from one of the houses. The windows had been flung wide open so everyone could hear. Hitler was making a fiery speech—a war-cry of exultant frenzy because Japan had caught a lot of United States warships by surprise and sunk them so that thousands of sailors must be drowned. As Hitler's powerful voice rose to a crescendo of wild defiance, Eric pulled his ear-tabs down tighter and hurried on toward Hameln. Would the whole world burn and bleed and perhaps be destroyed in this awful war?

Eric stopped in the middle of the road. A disturbing thought had come to him. Suppose Father had stayed in the United States? Then he would have been an American boy! Would he be somebody different? No, of course not. He'd still be Eric Kreye. He went on toward Hameln, but he began to understand more what Father meant. Men who fought wars were really fighting against themselves, because if they'd been born in some other village— War never seemed the same to Eric again.

Four days later when the United States made formal declaration of war on Germany and Italy, demonstrations of German power took on a new dimension. The Nazi youth leaders whipped their young followers into a fury of excitement which seemed, even to Eric, to be compounded of hatred and fear. More and more Father's ideas came to be his own.

Now when Father suggested that he stay away from *Jungvolk* meetings because farm work had become too pressing, or because Father needed him to help in the *Gasthaus* bar, he felt relieved.

Eric looked at the calendar—December 11th—only thirteen days till Christmas Eve. He tried to put all thoughts of war and bombings out of his mind. He tried to forget the freezing Russian winter and the splendid *Wehrmacht* soldiers on the eastern front. Christmas, the happiest time of the whole year in the Kreye home, would be here in thirteen days.

A week before Christmas the excitement began. Father cut a big pine tree and carried it into the parlor. Little Irmgard watched him with big wondering eyes. Even Eric felt a tremendous thrill to see that big tree being carried into the parlor.

Mother kept the door locked, but the whole house seemed to shiver with joy over the things Father did behind that locked door. The children could only listen to Father humming a tune as he worked. Eric knew that wonderful preparations went on in the parlor, but the children would not see any of the presents or the sparkly, glittery things until Christmas Eve.

He and Irmgard followed Mother around the kitchen begging to help while she worked her magic with cakes, cookies, candies, bread, and other delicacies.

"When did people begin to have Christmas trees?" Irmgard asked while she and Eric watched Mother shape the sugar roof of a little Christmas cottage—a fruitcake.

32

"Some people say that the very first Christmas trees were used in Germany over four hundred years ago."

"Did they sing Christmas carols around the tree as we do?"

"Yes, Eric, some of the most beautiful carols were written and sung first of all here in Germany."

"Mother, will Sankt Nikolaus come to our house this year?"

"Wait and see. Have you been such a good boy that you want him to come?"

Eric thought back over the past months and didn't feel too sure that the good saint would approve his behavior. He couldn't forget the beatings he had gotten from Herr Meier or the trouble he'd had with the mayor when he built that fire last summer. He decided to say no more about Sankt Nikolaus, but he couldn't help wondering if the saint was a Nazi. Probably not. Sankt Nikolaus believed in having boys pray and go to church and be kind to everyone. Hitler believed only in fighting and war.

The gay and exciting days seemed to crawl while the children wondered if Christmas Eve would ever come.

When Eric awakened on the morning of December 24, he leaped out of bed, hurried into his clothes, and ran down to the kitchen shouting his delight all the way. Hans and Irmgard already sat at their places at the table.

"We are going to eat lightly today so you will have a good appetite for the Christmas goodies." Mother filled their plates; and Eric felt sure that no matter how much breakfast he ate, he would still have room for the feast that night.

He knew that Father had eaten his breakfast already and would be in the parlor now, putting the last ornaments on the tree. Eric and Irmgard took turns all morning trying to look through the keyhole, but they could see only bits of sparkle and glitter and green pine needles which made them even more eager for the day to pass.

33

About four in the afternoon Mother told them to get dressed for church. They must have time to walk to church in Holtensen for the Christmas service. Father and Mother did not go. Eric knew that while he and his brother and sister were gone to church his parents would carry the gifts into the parlor and spread the table with all the Christmas goodies.

Irmgard could not walk. She jumped, skipped, whirled, and danced all the way to the short service and back. Eric almost skipped with her, and even Hans hurried along faster than usual.

As they came down the hill from Holtensen, they could see the dark and silent village spread out before them in the dimness of cloud-filtered winter moonlight. Eric felt a sharp twinge of grief for the lights that used to be in every window. Now the blackout curtains revealed not a glimmer of candlelight.

He knew that a Christmas tree with candles and ornaments decorated every house in the village, but they were hidden now. Just like the kindness in people's hearts. The black war hides it, he thought.

The softly falling snow touched his cheeks gently. He breathed in the fresh cold air and took hold of Irmgard's hand.

Mother waited for the children in the kitchen and gave them each a plate of light food. "You are hungry after your walk to the church, and I don't want you so starved that you can think of nothing but food."

Supper finished, they crowded round the parlor door. Suddenly a bell rang out loud and clear. The sound seemed to come from outside. They all looked at each other. "I know who rang that bell," Eric said.

Father came up from the basement. "I heard it too. Who do you suppose it was?"

"Sankt Nikolaus maybe!" Irmgard danced up and down in glad excitement.

Mother unlocked the door, and they filed in, Irmgard first, then the rest of the family in the order of their ages.

Fragrance of pine rushed out to meet them. Candlelight dazzled their eyes. Eric knew that nothing in the world could be more beautiful than that Christmas tree. It touched the ceiling, and glistening ornaments and tinsel hung from every twig. It stood in front of a mirror almost as tall as the tree itself, and all its magnificence reflected back in doubled glory.

Then Eric's attention shifted to the long table with its snowy cloth. Piles of gifts had been stacked by each plate, while Christmas candy, cakes, and sweets of all kinds heaped the platters that crowded each other in the center of the table.

For a moment the children stood dazed by so much wealth and warmth and tender love springing up in this wonder of Christmas.

Then Father motioned them to sit on the floor while Mother read the Christmas story from the Bible. When she came to the words, "Peace on earth, goodwill toward men," she paused for a moment and looked at Father.

With a start, Eric realized what lay behind that quiet look that his parents exchanged. Something about it recalled to him his moment on the way home from church when he saw all the houses dark.

He could almost read their thoughts. The whole world struggled in the grip of a terrible war. The radio, silent now and covered with green boughs and holly berries, blared forth hate and defiance every day. Nations bared their teeth and snarled and tore at one another like savage wolves.

Mother paused only a moment. Then she smiled around on them all and went on with the story. Tonight they would enjoy another safe and joyous Christmas together. She finished the reading, and they sat around the tree singing Christmas carols until Mother told them that the time had come for the Christmas goodies. They devoured the many kinds of sweets with as much fervor as though they had been without food for days.

A thunderous knock sounded on the door and jerked everyone to instant attention. "Sankt Nikolaus! Sankt Nikolaus!" The children shouted and clapped their hands as the jolly bewhiskered fellow burst into the room with a huge pack on his back. After questioning the sober children, he rewarded them with gifts from his pack. Then, after admonishing them to be good and obedient during the coming year, he vanished in a flurry of snow and a tinkle of bells. Eric saw that he dragged a heavy iron chain behind him, and it made a solemn clank as it clattered over the frozen ground.

Now the servants, Ursula and Ludwig, came in, and Mother heaped plates with good things for them. Then everyone began to open the gifts. Eric forgot everything else in the pleasure of the suspenseful moment. When he saw Irmgard, Hans, Mother, Father, and the servants open their packages, his delight in his own gifts doubled, trebled, and quadrupled.

With hugs, kisses, and squeals of joy, the gifts were finally all opened and admired. The hands on the clock pointed to a late hour—much later than the children's usual bedtime. Gathering up their gifts, they all filed out. Father snuffed the candles, and for the first time in a week Eric felt tired. He followed Hans upstairs to their cold bedroom and snuggled under the feather bed. He must get a good rest tonight. Tomorrow they would have the great Christmas feast. He reached his feet for the hot-water bottle that Mother never forgot to provide, and then he fell into deep slumber.

 **four**

WINTER, 1942, SEEMINGLY COLDER than usual bore down hard on the warring nations of Europe. But the German people knew that something more than the cold increased their miseries. Rumors filtering back from the eastern front told of unexpected stubborn resistance from the Russian armies—of a *Wehrmacht* virtually frozen in its tracks along endless miles of desolated country. The people knew firsthand of increased demands for fighting men and the food and clothing to supply them.

Already scant rations were reduced as food became scarce. Mother had anticipated such a shortage, and rows of glass jars filled the cupboards in the basement storeroom. A number of food items came under government restriction: meat, grain, dairy products, potatoes, and other foods. Father had to plan with care because he had relatives in the large cities where life was hard. He must conserve food for them too.

"Eric, you must get up a little earlier in the morning to turn the cream separator," Father told him. "When Ursula finishes the milking, Mother will bring the pails of milk into the basement. I will show you how we can manage to keep enough whole milk for the family and some of the cream for churning." Father added in a lower voice, "When the inspector counted the cows, I think he missed a couple of them. Someone chased them to a far corner of the meadow."

"But Father—" Fear suddenly rose in Eric.

"My son," Father spoke in a solemn voice. "The law of God stands above the laws of men. We are working to save lives."

Eric knew that his father disliked to do unlawful things, but what else could he do?

Eric left his warm bed and went down to the basement in time to do his work before people began moving about on the street in front of the *Gasthaus* door. A bus came along at six-thirty, and passengers who must wait for the bus often stepped inside the *Gasthaus* restaurant to get out of the cold.

"I think this separator must make more noise than any other machine in Unsen," Eric said to Mother one morning when she brought in the milk. "Hitler would surely have the *Gestapo* after me if he knew about this separator."

"But you are early, Eric." Mother set the pails of milk down by the separator. "No one is going past our house so early in the morning."

"I hope they aren't, but just the same it scares me. I don't feel right going against what Hitler says."

"We want to live, Eric." Mother spoke in a low voice. "We want to save the lives of other people who are dear to us. You must help us, Eric."

Mother went to bring the big milk can, for they must set it out by the road for the dairy wagon from Hameln to pick up.

Eric began to turn the noisy cream separator. He knew that Father and Mother were willing to give their lives so that their family might have food. What kind of coward was he anyway?

Father had always taught Eric to obey God, his parents, and the laws of the Fatherland. Now Father and God seemed to be going in the opposite direction from Hitler. He felt confused, but he made a firm decision to go with God and with Father.

He turned the separator with growing fright. Each loud whine seemed to cry out, "Come, come! Look at this boy. He is separating cream to make butter. Look! Look! He is a traitor!"

At last he finished. He knew that Mother waited for him in the kitchen. "Eric, you are a good boy." She took the pan of cream from his unsteady hands. She had already set out the churn, and Eric knew that they had already saved enough cream to make a big lump of butter today. "What would we do without you, Eric?" Mother fed him a good breakfast, and he started for school.

In the streets of Holtensen Eric found a number of people gathered round a posted notice that a soldier had just fastened to a tree. He pressed through the crowd and read the big black words:

> *Sheltering of enemy aliens will from this date be punishable with death.*

He didn't wait to read more. Fear flashed through his body like an electric shock. "Enemy alien!" Who could that mean? Then as he listened to the talk on the street and at school, he realized that the "enemy aliens" were Jews! Later he heard the fierce voice of Adolf Hitler in a radio broadcast:

> *We intend to wage this war until the Jews have been wiped off the face of the earth."*

But the German Jews weren't aliens. Many of them came from families that had lived in Germany for hundreds of years. How could Hitler be at war with the Jews? One of Eric's favorite aunts was a Jewess.

Then Eric thought of Professor Stoll and his Jewish wife. They had stayed at the *Gasthaus* for a week not long ago, and he'd heard Father say that they would come back in a few days and spend a month or two, maybe longer. Now what would Father do? Would he send them away? Would he report them to the *Gestapo?*

Eric's hands shook, and throughout that day he felt too restless to study. He hurried home when his lessons were ended, and he didn't feel like playing with Volker and Frevie although they both waited for him in Holtensen.

He stood at the kitchen door for a moment listening to Mother whistling at her work. She always whistled when she worked about the house. Eric hadn't thought much about it before, but now the sound of Mother's whistling comforted him like a soothing hand. He walked in.

"You are home, Eric!" Mother always said those words with such gladness as though she had waited all day for this special moment. "Father has something special for you to do tonight. Go and change your clothes."

Some of the fear Eric had felt that morning while turning the cream separator, and later in Holtensen when he read Hitler's new law, came back now. He felt sure that whatever thing Father wanted him to do tonight would be another frightening adventure.

After supper Father asked Eric to follow him out to the barn. They went through the basement and along the covered passageway that led to the barn and the sheds. Father took him into one of the storage rooms where gunny sacks hung at every window. He looked around and saw other things.

41

Father said, "We are going to kill our biggest pig tonight. You will be our guard and lookout."

"Father," he said, "this place looks like a butcher shop."

"That's exactly what it's going to be for tonight. We are going to kill our biggest pig tonight. You will be our guard."

Eric felt his legs tremble. "But Father, the pig will squeal!"

"Yes, it will, Son; but we must take the chance. In wartime we have to do many strange things. We have relatives in Hamburg, in Gütersloh, and in Bad Pyrmont who will go hungry unless we can take them food." He laid his hand on Eric's shoulder. "When any law tells us to do wrong, or forbids us to do right, then we disobey that law. Do you understand?"

Eric understood. Late in the night Father roused him from his troubled sleep. He put on his warmest clothing and went down to the basement and through the covered passageway to the barn. He found that a friendly neighbor had come to do the butchering. Eric knew that the man had long experience in the butchering trade. A couple of other men had come too—men whom Father trusted. Ludwig must be asleep in his room. The hired help must never know of these secret goings-on. They could not be trusted. The huge pig was already in the room Eric had seen earlier in the evening.

"Our lives are in your hands," Father told Eric. "Keep careful watch clear to the end of the street in both directions. Hide yourself. Don't let anyone see you."

Eric took up his watch. He knew that no person could be trusted. Everyone was encouraged to report any unlawful acts among their own families and their neighbors' families. His hands felt damp inside his mittens. The cold bit through his thick clothing, but he scarcely noticed it.

He looked at the barn. Not a glimmer of light showed through the draped windows. Wait! was that a shadow down by the Rasche farm? It moved— Only a dog! His heart began to beat again.

42

A few sounds came from the barn, but nothing that could startle anyone. Then it came—a loud and piercing squeal, shrill, high, and long-drawn-out!

Eric's heart almost leaped from his body. He put both hands to his mouth to hold it in. For a moment he felt as though he had received the fatal stroke instead of the big pig.

Then he looked in every direction. No doors opened; no window rattled. All the houses of Unsen lay quiet under the winter moon. Not a shadow moved in all the snowy landscape.

Surely no pig had ever died so noisy a death. Yet the sounds that seemed so loud to Eric failed to arouse anyone in the sleeping village. Even Frau Schmidt and her Nazi son, Otto, must be sleeping unusually well tonight.

Father came out of the barn. "You may go to bed now, Son. You are a good boy. You have kept faithful watch. The rest of the work we must do will make no noise."

When Eric came downstairs the following morning, he found Mother in the basement with two huge kettles over the fires. One kettle contained cans of meat and the other, potatoes.

The Kreye family had their own canning outfit and preserved the meat in tin cans just like those in the stores. Eric thought they were lucky to have such equipment. Now whenever they processed meat they always cooked large kettles of potatoes for the hogs. The smell of the potatoes seemed to cover the tell-tale odor of cooking meat from an occasional burst can.

Eric went back upstairs determined to keep a sharp watch for any persons who might look suspicious. He felt somehow that Hitler must have heard that pig squeal in Berlin, and he might be able to smell the meat cooking too.

That day was a holiday, and before long Father came in and told Eric to get dressed in his warm clothes. "We have some digging to do," he said. "We will do it inside the buildings where the ground is not frozen so hard."

They dug a deep trench in the machine shed. Not a crumb of fresh dirt could be left lying about. Eric had to haul it to the creek and sprinkle it along the edge where it would not show.

They dug another trench in the wood shed. They worked hours, and they must do it all secretly; not even the servants, Ursula or Ludwig, must know about the plans they were making.

Eric remembered that last fall a big pile of potatoes had been hidden under a trash heap behind the barn. No one knew about that either. All the burying must be done by night.

When the deep trenches were finished at last, Father and Eric carried out the cans of meat and hid them. They took large glass containers and put the cans inside so that no dampness could rust the cans. They covered them with care. They laid boards over the trench and scattered straw thick over the floor. When morning came, the mower stood in its place, and the neat stacks of firewood filled the rearranged wood shed. No one would imagine that so much valuable food lay concealed under those innocent covers.

Father now laid plans to carry food to Aunt Johanne and her family in Gütersloh. Eric thought of Cousin Gertrud. He hoped she was not too hungry. Father filled two suitcases with both fresh and canned meat, a few pounds of butter, and some oil. Eric tried to lift the suitcases, but in spite of his strong muscles he found them too heavy.

"I will take Irmgard with me," Father told Mother. "People will think that I have the little one's clothing in the suitcases. Maybe I will have a better chance of getting through."

five

ERIC SAW HIS FATHER GO off toward the train station in Hameln with the heavy suitcases. Little Irmgard clung to one of them because Father had no hand to hold her. He needed both hands to carry the heavy luggage.

Irmgard laughed and waved good-bye, glad because she could go with Father. They must ride the bus that stopped at the *Gasthaus* door. Eric stood with Mother watching them board the bus; and he realized how dangerous a trip this one might be. They caught a flash of Irmgard's yellow braids and one little hand in a last wave of joy. Eric knew Irmgard had no notion of why she had been allowed to go.

He looked at Mother. Her face had paled, and she ran into the house quickly. Eric thought he saw tears in her eyes, but half an hour later he heard her whistling as she tidied the *Gasthaus* kitchen and did her usual morning work.

A day passed—and another day. The family waited. Father should have come back by now, and Eric could see that Mother worried. But she tried to encourage the boys. "God will take care of him. You mustn't be afraid."

On the third day Father returned with Irmgard and the empty suitcases. They all welcomed him with such relief and affection that Father declared he had no idea he would be so much missed. Eric thought he could never endure having Father make that trip again.

After the travelers had changed their clothes and the suitcases had been stowed away, Mother asked, "What did you do, and why were you a day late?"

"I'll tell you all about it." Father sat at the table with the family around him. "When we got to the eastern suburb of Bielefeld, an air-raid siren began to scream, and of course the train stopped. The engineer refused to take it into the city."

"Did you have to wait long?"

"No, Eric, I lugged my two suitcases clear down to the main part of Bielefeld where I could catch a train for Gütersloh. Irmgard hung tight to one of them all the way." He drew Irmgard into his arms. "The little one got rather tired, but she is a good little guard." He sighed and pressed his face against Irmgard's yellow hair. "I feared every moment that someone would take the suitcases from me and discover the food I carried in them. Then, of course, I would be in jail now."

"I suppose Aunt Johanne and Uncle Heinrich and Cousin Gertrud needed the food."

"Yes, Eric, when I saw how much they needed it and how thankful they were, all my worry and trouble seemed nothing." Father paused and Eric saw a determined look in his eyes. "We must not disappoint them. We are the only ones who have ways of getting food to them."

Then Eric knew that Father must go again. Several times that winter he made the trip to Gütersloh and each time he carried a heavy load of food. Each trip became more dangerous as food restrictions tightened and penalties of greater severity were enforced.

Eric did guard duty for Father's butchering again and again before spring came.

Mother made food-carrying trips too. Her parents and her younger sister Hildegard lived in Bad Pyrmont, and she took them bread, meat, and cooking fat. Sometimes Grandma came to visit at the *Gasthaus* and carried away food with her. Aunt Hildegard pulled a little trailer behind her bicycle, and she came almost every week to get potatoes. She often stayed to help about the house and garden, for Mother had more work than she could handle looking after her family and the guests.

Spring came again, and wild flowers bloomed in the woods. Now Eric gathered wild strawberries in the meadow pasture at the edge of the forest. One day Mother made strawberry shortcake, and she set a big pitcher of cream on the table. (No one was allowed to have cream. Hitler had forbidden it.)

Just as the family began to enjoy the delicious shortcake and the fresh cream, a loud knock on the door disturbed them. Eric ran out to find their neighbor Otto Schmidt. He wondered if any marks of the shortcake or the forbidden cream might be showing around his mouth. Otto seemed to notice nothing unusual. He had come on a harmless errand, but when Eric returned to the table he pushed the dish of unfinished short-cake away. "It doesn't taste good, Mamma," he said. "Don't make any more. It's too mixed with danger."

That afternoon Herr Stoll arrived at the *Gasthaus* with his wife and daughter. Eric held his breath waiting to see what Father would do.

He welcomed them with the same courtesy that he showed all his guests and showed them to their room on the second floor. After a few days Professor Stoll left, but his wife and their daughter, Rosemarie, stayed.

Now new peril menaced the Kreye household. Killing pigs

at night and hiding the meat, running the cream separator before daylight, and churning butter had been terrifying enough; but now the Kreye family added another unlawful action to the rather long list. They sheltered an "enemy alien."

Father never told Eric not to speak of these illegal acts and situations. He trusted his family without laying a single restriction on them. Eric thought of his Jewish aunt and hoped that some kind person would protect and shelter her if the need should arise. Slowly but with terrible sureness, resistance had rooted and grown in Eric's mind until he would rather die than reveal any of the unlawful happenings in his father's house.

On a pleasant summer day Eric, Volker, and Frevie marched toward Holtensen to attend a *Jungvolk* meeting. "Today we are going to gather herbs and seeds for our *Führer*," Volker said. "I think they will be used for medicine—for soldiers."

At the schoolhouse the boys separated into teams, each with a leader. Under the leader's direction they scattered through the woodland, alert for plants that might be useful. The leader held several samples in his hands, and the boys ran back to him every few minutes to compare some plant they had found.

Eric looked around the forest glade with keen eyes. He'd never realized how many valuable and useful things grew wild in the woods.

When they returned to the exercise ground at Holtensen, the boys piled the sacks of herbs and plants in a heap—quite an imposing pile. Their leader had taught them some valuable things about plants. Now he held up his hand for attention. "A new rule has been made for all *Jungvolk*," he told the boys. "From now on, beechnuts will be redeemed by our government for margarine and cooking oil."

"Heil Hitler!" they all shouted.

"I wonder how long it'll take us to gather a pound of those nuts. They're so small," Frevie said.

On the way home, the boys found some beechnuts. As Frevie had said, they were tiny, about half an inch long and shaped like a teardrop with three ridges on it.

"I wonder what they will use them for." Eric held some of the nuts in his hand.

"I know." Volker explained that his father had seen the machines that the government used to press the oil from the beechnuts. "It is good for cooking. I suppose they want it for the army."

That summer and fall the boys gathered things from the forest that they had never hunted before. Eric collected many pounds of the tiny beechnuts, and in return he got precious oil which Father took to Aunt Johanne and Uncle Heinrich in Gütersloh and to other dear ones in other cities.

The boys gathered different kinds of mushrooms, the white-topped ones with pink gills that grew in the open meadows and pastures, the clumps of bright yellow ones that lived in the deep woods, and the big gray stone mushrooms that liked moist shady places along the creek banks.

The government had issued food ration stamps. Without these stamps one could not buy many necessary foods such as oil, margarine, sugar, flour, and meat. Even with the food stamps many of the city people never had enough food. In Unsen the Kreye family had their basement storeroom stocked with canned fruit and vegetables. They had their own milk and meat. They had grain which they could have ground into meal or flour.

Father often told them, "We work hard, but we are better off than most people."

Because the *Gasthaus* restaurant had a bar, and because Mother served excellent home-cooked meals, Nazi leaders sometimes held their meetings there. Almost all the neighbors respected Father as a fine, patriotic gentleman; but sometimes

49

the Nazis who attended these meetings behaved in such a greedy and boisterous manner that Eric heard Father condemn them in private as "pigs."

One evening four gentlemen came from Hameln to eat supper in the *Gasthaus* dining room. One of them Eric recognized as a teacher, the others he had never seen before. The men drank liquor along with their meal, and they grew more and more hilarious as the evening advanced. Finally at a late hour one of them called to Father, "Herr Kreye, come and join us here at our table. We want to talk to you."

Father sat down with them, and the five of them began to discuss politics. Hitler's *Wehrmacht* seemed to be in a difficult position on the eastern front again. Father, who thought the whole Hitler plan a bunch of deadly nonsense, drank with the men and began to express his opinions with unusual freedom. He supposed these other gentlemen felt as he did about Hitler. He referred to the "Hitler gang" as *"das Gemüse"* (the vegetables—a term of derision).

One of the men bristled with anger, and Father realized that he had offended a dangerous Nazi fanatic. The threatening situation startled him, and he talked with all the diplomacy and tact he could muster to extricate himself from the dangerous predicament. He exerted all his charm. The session ended two hours later with Father completely sober and thankful beyond measure for deliverance from what might have been certain death.

"Remember, boys," he told Eric and Hans the next day, "liquor and politics do not mix well. Never befuddle your brains, because your tongue is fastened into your head too."

A few weeks later when Father was ordered to present himself for *Gestapo* training, he went unwillingly, but he dare not refuse, because he did not know what lay behind the summons. For three months he trained for the secret police, but at the

51

Suddenly Father realized that he had offended a dangerous Nazi fanatic!

end of that time he got permission to return to his farm.

One morning in October Eric watched Hans put on his *Hitler-Jugend* uniform. He dressed with unusual care and checked his appearance in front of the mirror. Eric thought he had never seen a finer looking fellow than his brother Hans. Dressed in his neat uniform, he looked splendid. Eric asked him, "Where are you going today, Hans?"

"To Bückeberg near Hameln." Hans twisted his neck to get his tie on just right. "I will see Hitler and hear him speak."

"Oh, that's what they do every year in Bückeberg, isn't it? Thousands of people come there every October."

"Hundreds of thousands," Hans corrected. "Maybe a million." Hans started for the door.

"Oh, Hans, let me go with you." Eric had heard of the great outdoor convention held each October in Bückeberg where the farmers and other people gathered from all over Germany. He had never gone. Father didn't seem to think it important.

"Of course you can't go. This celebration is not for children. Only men will be there."

Eric listened to Hans's quick step on the stairs. Why did Hans always talk to him as if he were a small child?

All that day Eric thought about Hans and all the wonderful things he must be seeing and hearing.

At the supper table that evening Mother asked, "Did you have a good day, Hans?"

"Oh, yes, Mother!" Hans looked as if he had seen a vision of glory. "Thousands—hundreds of thousands of people came. Hitler, Goebbels, Baldur von Schirach, and others of our great leaders stood on the platform all decorated with flags." Hans paused as though even the memory of it overwhelmed him. "Oh, Mother, you should have seen the flags all around the base of the mountain like a fence."

Eric shut his eyes and tried to imagine what the convention had looked like with all those flags—red, bright red, with the round white circle and the black swastika in the center. Surely no flag could be so beautiful as the flag of the Third Reich. He tried to picture thousands of flags, enough to make a fence around Bückeberg mountain.

Hans continued his story. "They had built a whole village of cardboard, but it looked real. You should have seen our tanks attack! You should have heard the *Stukas* screech when they dived! You should have seen the Storm Troopers march! They demolished that village in a moment of time, it seemed. It blazed up in a beautiful fire."

Hans stood up, and a lofty look spread over his handsome face. "Just so our *Wehrmacht* will destroy every village in Russia, every village in England, and," he looked at Father, "every village in any other country that dares oppose our *Führer.*"

Father dropped his fork beside his plate and a desolate look came over his face. He regarded his older son, as he often did these days, with pity in his eyes. He left the table and went out into the autumn evening. Eric had a curious feeling that something very sad had happened, but he couldn't explain what it was.

One afternoon a few days later as Eric played in the *Gasthaus* garden, he looked down and saw some food ration stamps at his feet. Someone must have dropped them while walking between the flowerbeds. He picked them up. Ration stamps meant butter, meat, sugar, and other things that had become scarce in Germany these last months. The pangs of hunger pinched everyone now. Even in Unsen people felt it, and in the big cities so many suffered hunger that Eric couldn't bear to think about it.

Something fluttered past his eyes, and he saw more ration

stamps lying on the grass. These stamps must be coming from the sky. Could they be real? Now he saw a few more beside the *Gasthaus*.

Eric gathered up a handful and took them into the house to show Mother. "Do you think they are true ration stamps?"

"They look all right to me, Eric," Mother said. "Why don't you take them over to the baker? He will know."

In the baker's shop Eric laid the stamps on the counter. "Sir, I found these in our garden. I even found a few here by your shop. Are they good food stamps?"

With a startled look the baker reached for them. He examined them with care. "No, Eric, I think they are counterfeit; but they are made so cleverly that they might fool some people."

"Where did they come from?"

"Allied planes must have dropped them."

"How can they make our ration stamps?"

"I don't know. Someone must have sneaked some of them out of Germany, and they copied them in England or America." The baker laid the food stamps back on the counter. "You are a good boy, Eric. I will call the police, and they will warn the people about these false ration stamps."

Eric left the baker's shop feeling proud and important. He had done a service for the Fatherland.

Christmas came again, but now the peace of Unsen suffered nightly disturbance from flights of bombers winging overhead on their way to targets in eastern Germany.

Then one evening early in 1943 Eric looked out the window toward the northeast over the Süntel and saw a red glow in the sky. He called the whole family. They grabbed warm clothing and ran out in the road in front of the *Gasthaus* to watch the fiery wonder grow and spread until the sky over the mountain blazed with light.

"Hannover!" Father caught his breath with a quick sound like a sob. "They are bombing Hannover!"

The flaming menace in the sky could mean nothing else. Even as they watched, they saw the upthrust of powerful searchlight beams. They could hear the distant rattle of anti-aircraft fire and the rumble of exploding bombs muffled by the distance. Then suddenly a burst of flame erupted just over the Süntel, and they saw a plane arch toward the ground leaving a flaming trail. Then, with a harsh and mournful wail, it spun around like a mortally wounded bird and spiraled faster and faster until the mountain hid its final death plunge.

Shivering with anxiety more than cold, the Kreye family went back into their comfortable home. For a moment no one spoke. Eric could feel that something had changed. Father had told them that when the United States came into the war the bombing attacks would be stepped-up. This night bombing planes had attacked Hannover less than thirty miles away!

Would the war planes come to Unsen too? Eric felt sure that they would. The wail of the dying airplane still whined in his ears. He had never heard such a sad, such a terrifying sound.

Father finally spoke. "It is sad that our cities must be destroyed in this way, but I can't see that the Allies have any other choice. Hannover has many likely targets: heavy industry, oil installations, and railway yards."

Now everything seemed to move faster. More bombers appeared in the skies. Fleets of warplanes streamed over the pleasant valley where Eric lived. More regulations began to affect the Kreye family.

Although newscasts over the radio announced a constant series of victories for Hitler's *Wehrmacht,* the flaming sky told the country people that while the *Luftwaffe* (German air

55

force) might be pounding enemy cities, Allied bombers streaked across the Fatherland almost every night to leave a trail of blazing destruction.

As the winter wore on, news from Russia became so discouraging that nothing Hitler could say concealed the catastrophe that had engulfed the Sixth Army at Stalingrad on the Volga. From listening to foreign broadcasts, Father knew that General Paulus and his troops had run into desperate trouble. Russian troops had closed in on them from two sides.

One January morning Eric saw that Father seemed to be shocked with grief. His face looked gray and his eyes sunken as though he hadn't slept for a long time. He wondered what could have happened to distress Father so much. Eric followed him to the barn to help with the morning chores.

"Father, did you hear some bad news over the radio?"

"I heard that Hitler has just squandered three-hundred-thousand men with General Paulus in Stalingrad." His eyes blazed with grievous hurt and furious anger. "Hitler is mad!"

Eric learned later how the *Führer* had refused to let General Paulus save his men while retreat was still possible and had issued his order, "Victory or death!" So the soldiers had died— almost all of them. Only a few had been taken prisoner.

Now the tide of battle rolled back over the hundreds of miles which the *Wehrmacht* had wrested from Russia. City after city was retaken, and when summer lay again on the tortured land, refugees from the eastern front began to appear in the villages of the valley where Eric lived.

"Must we feed them?" Mother asked Father. "There are so many, and they are desperate, frightened people whose homes have been destroyed. They have nothing but the rags they are wearing."

Father considered the question. "Yes, we must feed all of them we can. War has made them what they are. What we can give seems so little for so many, but let us do what we can."

Not all the wandering people could be fed, and groups of them roamed the valley, sleeping out in the warm weather and stealing what food they could find.

One night the dog, Wolf, set up a loud barking behind the *Gasthaus*. Father stirred in his sleep. "Must be a cat." He raised up on his elbow and listened. "Yes, that squeaking noise is surely some prowling cat."

Next morning Eric found that the basement window right below his own upstairs window had been pried open. "Now I know what that squeaking noise was," he told Father.

They hurried down to the basement and found that thieves had taken a lot of Mother's canned fruit. They must have used some kind of metal bar to pry apart the expanded metal guard in the window.

"Look!" Eric pointed to a pile of prune pits. "They stopped right here and ate a whole jar of fruit." He kicked around in the shrubbery and found more pits. "Those rascals must have had a real feast—and right here where I could have looked down from my bedroom window and seen them!" Eric didn't know why, but those piles of fruit pits angered him more than anything else he had seen for a long time.

"Be patient, Son," Father said. "These people are starving. I am sure we shall have much more of this thieving. What can you expect when hundreds of thousands of people are robbed of everything they possess by a senseless war?"

The outlanders from the eastern borders of the Fatherland continued to come, and the government insisted that the village people take care of them. Some were sheltered in the *Gasthaus,* even on the third floor where no guests had been kept before. Mother fed crowds of refugees from her kitchen. Ursula helped her, and sometimes Aunt Hildegard came from Bad Pyrmont to work at preparing and handing out the food.

57

six

AUTUMN OF 1944 THREW darker shadows over the world and over Germany. Now, during daylight hours, Eric saw fleets of American bombers darken the sky over the valley where Unsen nestled among its gardens and meadows. And British bombers filled the night skies with terror.

To the boys already trained in war games and battle formation the sight of the enormous sweep of the big German bombers through the daytime skies in the early days of the war had seemed thrilling. Now, knowing the destruction and death these Allied bombers showered on German cities, Eric felt as Father did. Nothing about war made him glad or proud.

The air-raid alert sounded often these days, and the school children ran for the shelter a block away or, as Eric frequently did, leaped on their bicycles and pedaled for open country and home as fast as they could.

One day after Eric had left the school grounds and walked his bicycle a short distance, he heard the air-raid alert. He looked up and tried to count the bombers flying overhead.

They filled the sky like a shining river flowing east. Eric knew that each one of them carried a load of bombs for Berlin or other targets in northeastern Germany. The roar of their engines deafened him.

He realized that he had stopped right near the army barracks. Suppose one of those bombers decided to drop a bomb on those army barracks. He might not have much time.

He hurried to the air-raid shelter and found a lot of people already there. Most of them had become so accustomed to running for their lives that they had prepared packages of things they might need in the shelter. They also carried suitcases where they had packed their most valuable possessions. They grabbed these things when the air-raid alert sounded and raced to the protection of the underground bunker.

Eric hadn't thought much about air-raid shelters in the cities. At home the family ran for the basement if they felt it too dangerous to stay outside or upstairs. He had never been in the Hameln shelter before.

He looked at the people around him. Some of them lay on the floor. Others sat leaning against the cold walls of the bunker. "How long will this torment last?" one woman asked.

No one replied, because each one of them asked the same question in his mind.

"I wonder if our house will be hit today," one sad-looking woman with a baby in her arms remarked.

Again no one answered. Eric knew that all of them wondered the same thing.

A panicky voice shrilled above the others, "Will we be killed today?"

"Better for us if we are," a man's gruff voice replied. "Then we'll be out of our misery."

Eric looked at all the worried, tearful faces. He heard the

frightened children cry and saw the parents' desperate efforts to comfort them. He began to feel sick. The air in the bunker had become foul. He thought how lucky he was to have a home in the country where there were wide places to run and plenty of food and fresh air. He found himself panting to get out of the shelter.

Then a tremendous noise startled everyone. What could it be? Had a bomb struck the army barracks—a likely target? Had the Hameln school been hit?

The all-clear signal came at last, and Eric bounded out of the shelter and looked all around. He couldn't see any smoke or fire. Surely if the school or the army barracks had been hit there would be something to see.

He jumped on his bicycle and rode out of the city, all the time scanning wider and wider circles to discover what terrible thing had happened. Something big had been hit, he felt sure.

Then he saw it—a Flying Fortress down in a field at the edge of the city. German guards had begun to gather round it. There must be dead people inside that twisted mass of metal. With a rising sickness in his stomach he pedaled home.

Next morning before school he rode out to have another look at the wrecked plane. Only one soldier remained on guard this morning, and he stood on the other side of the wreckage with his face turned the other way.

Eric managed to loosen a few pieces of plexiglass, and he picked up a tracer bullet. He'd have fun with these things.

After school he rode through Holtensen looking for Volker and Frevie. He overtook them on the road home. He divided the plexiglass with them, and they agreed to meet later in the Kreye pasture where they set off the tracer bullet and enjoyed the display of fireworks.

One December evening Eric thought about the approaching Christmas season. He knew that Father and Mother would

60

Then he saw it—a Flying Fortress down in a field at the edge of the city.

have some surprises for the children. Mother had saved sugar, flour, and butter. He felt sure she had cookies in mind. Cookies had become a rare treat. Maybe Mother would even bake a fruitcake.

He knew that Father had already marked the pine tree he intended to cut. Pine trees grew in the woods about Unsen, and some of them were exactly right for Christmas trees. Next week Father would bring it in and decorate it with the ornaments which Mother always saved from year to year. She wrapped each one in soft paper and stored them in a big box in the attic.

The children had learned to value the old familiar bits of glitter, the spangled birds, gilded pendants, strings of shining balls, and festoons of tinsel. Eric remembered that the year before they had no silver icicles for their tree. He took out the soft wood he used for carving. He had almost finished a set of puppet heads for Irmgard. The heads were about the size of apples, and he set the finished ones out on the table in his room. Dresses could be made for each puppet and fastened with a tight string around a flange at the base of the heads. He had burned holes in the balls of wood so Irmgard could put her fingers inside them. They had much fun in the summertime with puppet shows. Sometimes they even charged a few *Pfennige* which the neighborhood children were always glad to pay.

Eric looked at the king's head and the queen's head. They seemed quite good, and he began to plan what kind of clothes they should have. Rosemarie knew how to make dresses for the puppets. Boys couldn't be expected to know about such things. Eric did know what colors he wanted, though. Color fascinated him.

The next morning as Eric walked along the street through the soft snow, he looked down at his feet and saw a bright shred of tinsel. What could have happened? He'd been thinking just the night before that they had no tinsel icicles this year. More tinsel fell. Then he saw that the air glistened with silver icicles as far and as high as he could see. They floated down like strange bright snowflakes.

He ran to call Irmgard, and together they collected all they could hold in their hands and went back for more. They smoothed it with loving care and tied it in bunches. At Christmastime they would have plenty of silver icicles on their tree.

"Who sent it?" Eric asked as he and Irmgard showed Father their tinsel.

"Allied planes must have dropped it." He looked at little Irmgard who held a bundle of the silver icicles to her breast as though it were a precious thing. "They drop it because these thin shreds of metal disturb radar."

For days after, Eric saw the tinsel scattered over the snowy fields and meadows, along the public roads, even on the housetops. He wondered why the big bombers sailing by the thousands through the skies over the Fatherland should think it worthwhile to drop these bits of silver tinsel to "disturb radar." Radar must be an important thing. Someday he'd find out about radar—someday when this war ended.

The need for food continued to distress the city dwellers. Eric could see the anxiety his parents felt for their relatives in the big cities. He knew that Hamburg had suffered many air raids. The gasoline refineries, the harbor, the railway yards, and the manufacturing plants offered many targets for Allied bombing. Now much of the city lay in ruins.

"We must get some food to Uncle Karl and Aunt Edith." Father sat by the kitchen table and looked at Mother with worried eyes. "They may be in desperate need. I'll have to go."

"No, it is too dangerous. You will surely be caught and imprisoned—perhaps executed." She clasped her hands tight to control their shaking. "Eric must go. He is so young. Perhaps people will not notice him. What else can we do?"

Father turned to Eric. "Son, are you willing to carry some food to your uncle and aunt in Hamburg? You know the danger." He clenched his fists. "What good are our lives to us if we allow our own flesh and blood to starve when we have food?"

Father got up and paced the kitchen floor. Eric could see his terrible anxiety, but he did not know whether it was for Uncle Karl and Aunt Edith or for himself—perhaps for the whole desperate situation.

Then Father came and put his hand on Eric's shoulder. "Maybe they will not suspect a schoolboy with a rucksack on his back."

The next day Father stood with Eric at the station in Hameln. He placed the heavy rucksack on Eric's back. "Do not be afraid, Son. Fear is a bad thing and makes a man look as if something is chasing him."

"Don't worry, Father. I will walk straight and with light feet as if the rucksack is stuffed with goose-down."

Eric saw the train coming. Father said good-bye and hurried toward home.

When the train came into the station, it looked so crowded that Eric decided to wait for the next one; but when it came, he could see that even more people had packed into it. They leaned out the windows and hung on the sides. Several trains went by, all of them crowded. Eric knew that if he expected to reach Hamburg that day he must push into the next one. So he forced his way into the train as he had seen others do.

He had to stand up. At least, he thought, there was no danger of falling. People wedged in so close about him that he could scarcely breathe. The heavy rucksack fastened about his shoulders pressed into his back. Cigarettes concocted from noxious weeds seemed to be in every passenger's mouth, and the smoke from them filled the air with a horrible stench. He wondered if he could endure the long trip to Hamburg.

The train pulled into another station, and Eric saw a lad about his own age trying to crowd into the coach. The boy carried a nice-looking suitcase which he handed in through the window. Several hands reached out to pull in the fine leather suitcase and then the boy. Before the new passenger could plant his feet on the floor, someone had jerked off his shoes and the suitcase had disappeared.

Eric felt the sickness in his stomach grow. What if he should faint? What would happen to the precious food he carried? What would become of him? The thought terrified him and made him feel worse. He gave a little gasp.

One of the passengers drew him over to an open window. "Rest here a little. You are tired of standing so long."

Eric came to himself with a violent start. Had he fainted? Had he been unconscious? For how long? He felt for his rucksack. Thank God! He could tell by its weight that no one had disturbed it.

When he got down from the train in Hamburg, he decided to walk to Aunt Edith's house. He knew it wasn't far, and he wanted to breathe the fresh air.

Could this city be Hamburg? Eric's eyes darted from rub- · ble heap to rubble heap, from desolation to desolation. What lay under the concealing snow, he could only imagine. Shaken and tired he marched in the direction of Aunt Edith's house. Would he find it standing when such awful destruction had wasted so much of the city? Maybe Aunt Edith and Uncle Karl weren't even alive!

Eric had started from Unsen in the early morning. The sunset glowed along the western sky when he knocked on Aunt

65

Edith's door. The area around her home had not yet been hit by bombs.

Aunt Edith threw the door open and welcomed Eric with surprise and affection. "Oh, Eric, how you have grown! What a brave boy you are to come all the way from Unsen."

Eric took off his rucksack and set it on the floor. "A little food for you," he said.

She lifted it to the table. "Eric! What a heavy load. How could you carry it all that way? And the danger— What if someone had discovered what you were carrying?" He saw the glisten of unshed tears in her eyes.

When Uncle Karl came home for supper and saw meat on the table and butter for his bread, the look on his face repaid Eric many times over for all the danger and terror of the trip.

"Uncle Karl," Eric asked, "do bombers come every night?"

"No, not every night, but often enough, my boy. They came last night. We know they are after military targets, but those block-busters don't pick and choose. They fall on lots of homes too."

Eric didn't sleep well that night. In his dreams he saw bombers roar across the sky like swarming bees, and under them the cities turned to twisted wire and metal and broken brick. In his dreams he heard the wail of countless air-raid sirens and heard the sobbing of children and the wailing of women. He saw the sky blaze and smelled the smoke of burning buildings.

He wakened at last, and Uncle Karl put him on a train that would take him home to Unsen. Again he felt his heart swell in a great surge of thankfulness for his country home. Then the swell rolled back in a crest of anger at the injustice and wickedness of war. Father's words rang in his ears, "War is hell!" He wondered how human beings could deliberately choose to inflict such horror on their fellowmen.

66

He walked into the kitchen at home that evening, and Mother looked at him. "Oh, Eric, you are home!" Her face lighted up with relief and pride. "You are a good, brave boy. Now tell us about your trip to Hamburg."

The family gathered around the supper table and listened to Eric describe his journey, but for some reason there seemed little to tell. All that he had seen and felt in the last thirty-six hours millions of other people were seeing and feeling every day. His own small terror and grief seemed over-shadowed —caught up in the darkness of a world horror which he had just begun to comprehend.

"Hannover suffered another heavy raid last night," Father said. "I think the end must not be far away."

Later when Eric went to the barn with Father to help with the chores, Father told him about the Battle of the Bulge and how it had ended. "And the Russians have opened a massive offensive on our eastern border," Father went on. "Already they are on German soil." Father explained how he had learned all this news from listening to the London broadcast over the big brown radio in the parlor.

Eric looked at the solid stone walls of the barn and thought of the thick brick walls of his father's house and wondered how long before a bomb would fall close enough to shatter the *Gasthaus* to a mass of broken brick and tile.

seven

ERIC GOT LITTLE SCHOOLING that winter. Although the teachers tried to conduct classes, they were so often interrupted by the air-raid sirens that sometimes school lasted but an hour or less.

As winter began to melt into early spring, Hitler issued an order for all able-bodied men between the ages of fifty-one and sixty to join the armed forces.

Father disregarded this order and continued on his little farm. He lamented that Hitler had wasted over a million men—the flower of the German youth—in Russia.

Now the *Luftwaffe* appeared no more in force in the skies. The deadly *Stukas* and *Messerschmitts* sat on the ground helpless. Many of the young pilots who had hurled such planes into English skies to rain fury on English cities occupied hero's graves. There were no pilots to take their places.

Recruiters appeared in Hameln and Holtensen. With brave speeches and patriotic war cries, they urged the youngsters in the *Hitler-Jugend* to come to the aid of the Fatherland in one final push to glorious victory.

Hans needed no urging. Hitler had long been his hero, and he followed his *Führer* without question. The whole family grieved to see him go marching away with his fellow youth. Where would they go? What was their future? Nobody could foresee.

Eric often caught a look of desperate sadness in Mother's eyes, but she did her work about the farm and the house with unfailing patience, thankful that Father did not have to go to the front. The increasing food shortage demanded that farmers of Father's status keep on producing as much as possible.

One afternoon in spring Eric and his two friends put a few washed potatoes in their pockets and went up on the hillside where they intended to build a fire and have a potato roast. Volker gathered tiny twigs and dead tree branches while Eric and Frevie cleared a good place to build a fire. They let the fire burn for quite a while; then they prepared a bed of hot coals and dropped the potatoes into the ashes. Eric heard the sound of a plane.

He looked up and recognized it as a P-38. Everyone dreaded the P-38's because they moved so fast that nothing could get away from one if it decided to give chase.

The boys dashed up the hillside and then turned to look back. Eric saw an army truck just entering Unsen. "Look, the P-38 is after that truck!" He grabbed Frevie by the shoulder. "See it dive!"

Two times the pursuit plane dived low over the truck and strafed it with all its guns. The truck stopped, and the boys started to run down the hill. There must be soldiers in that truck—German soldiers.

As they got nearer Eric could see several soldiers hiding in the ditch beside the road. The boys hurried until they stood by the truck. Then they saw that it carried office equipment; beautiful desks, cabinets, chairs, files, and other things. All of

69

it had been riddled with machine-gun fire. Nothing in the truck could be worth a *Pfennig* except perhaps for kindling wood.

Three sober boys went back to their homes. They had forgotten all about the potato roast.

That spring few of the farmers could plow their land. They could sow no seed. So suddenly and so swiftly did enemy planes sweep out of the skies that no living thing was safe anywhere in the fields, pastures, or meadows.

"I think Hitler is about finished," Father said one day in April. "For a long time the Allies have been attacking the heavy industry, the oil refineries, and the railway centers." Then he told them how Allied bombers had almost obliterated Germany's chief source of oil—the great refining plant at Ploesti far back in conquered Rumania. The great munition manufacturing plants had suffered massive damage.

Eric had seen for himself the destruction in Hamburg, and the fire in the sky over the Süntel had become so common that they had come to accept it as a regular occurrence.

Refugees from both east and west continued to come in large numbers. As the defenses of the Fatherland crumbled and the Allied armies drove deeper into German territory, the government diverted the refugees into areas where they might find enough food to keep them alive until something happened. Father explained it to Eric.

But what could happen now? Russian armies pushed in from the east. Allied armies pressed toward the German heartland from the west. Hitler and his boastful generals had holed-up in his bunker in Berlin, Father supposed, although no one seemed to know for sure.

Eric watched the ragged, weary, discouraged lines of people that straggled through the *Gasthaus* gardens. He saw how Mother and Aunt Hildegard and Ursula worked to provide nourishing soup and bread for them. Then they passed on and other suffering people took their places.

One woman from Aachen spent a few days in the third story of the *Gasthaus*. So shattered were her nerves that even a spring thundershower would send her flying down the three flights of stairs to the basement where she would huddle in whimpering terror. Eric could only guess at what the poor woman must have been through to make her panic at the sound of thunder.

On a spring evening Eric came into the kitchen and found everything quiet. Not a good kind of quiet, he thought. Father looked grave, and Eric could see that Mother had been crying.

"Oh, Eric, Hans is shot!" Irmgard ran to him and hung to his hand sobbing. Eric felt something inside him twist into a hard knot. He could not speak.

"A man came to tell us today," Father explained. "He said that Hans was working with other young lads at preparing our defense lines up on the Elbe. Enemy planes came over and killed most of the boys in the company." He hesitated, seemed to take a firmer grip on his emotions and went on. "Now, I don't think we should give up hope. The man didn't see Hans shot. Maybe he got away. We will pray God he did."

Eric could see that Mother took no comfort from Father's good words and that Father himself had little hope that he would see his strong handsome son again.

Now each night as Eric looked at Hans's empty bed, he felt the grief grow in his heart until he found it hard to remember that he had ever been young or happy. The leaves came out on the beech trees. New grass carpeted the meadow, and flowers sprang up even where machine guns had torn the black soil with destruction.

The renewed beauty of nature seemed to be trying to tell

him something, but he couldn't figure what it was. Perhaps he still grieved too much about Hans. Maybe he had become too weary of war and its continual strain. Could the sweet sights and sounds of springtime be only a hypocritical smile that concealed some deadly threat?

Now the stealing of food became a common occurrence. Hungry people closed in from every direction. The bombing began to come closer, even as close as Hameln. The German army had formed pockets of resistance where soldiers disputed every square foot of German soil and drenched it with their blood before surrendering it to the invaders. When bombs began to fall on Hameln, and artillery shells over-shot their mark in the direction of Unsen, the Kreye family, and all the people in the *Gasthaus,* hurried to the basement.

The Jewish lady, Frau Stoll, brought her small daughter, Rosemarie, and put her in the coal bin because she had contracted scarlet fever.

Each burst of shell-fire seemed louder and nearer than the last. So close were the detonations that a sudden shift of air-pressure flicked out every candle in the basement and struck terror to Eric's heart.

The refugees crowded into the darkened room began to moan and wail. They had fled their bombed-out homes only to meet the frightful thing in Germany's heartland where they had expected to be safe. They cried that they had no way to escape, no refuge, no protection.

The shells fell so close that the walls seemed ready to collapse and fall in on them. In that terrible moment Eric felt such a need of God as he had never known before. Father and Mother had taught him about God from early childhood, but now at this awful moment he needed to know for himself that behind all the terror and the noise, behind all the destruction in the world, God still existed. Surely somewhere

72

there must be an answer of peace to all this frightful fear and grief. But no answer came.

Eric felt sure that this day must be the last day of his life, and he knew that the most important thing must be to understand that God cares. God cares even for terrified boys in basements being bombed and shelled.

At last the hideous noise subsided into silence, and the people could hear little Rosemarie crying softly in the coal bin.

They knew that the attack on Hameln must be over. They came up out of the basement and found the *Gasthaus* still standing. They walked out into the streets of Unsen where they found their neighbors wandering about as dazed as themselves.

For five years this murderous and desperate war had plagued the Fatherland, first by taking young men away to die in distant lands. Now even small villages like Unsen in country places suffered constant fear. All the inhabitants lived every day in terror of death from the skies. Now, added to the accumulated terror of the past five years, loomed this new anguish.

The Kreye family suffered fear of discovery because of the food situation—the pigs they must butcher during the darkest hours of night, the cream that must be separated before dawn with the squeakiest separator in all Germany.

Father took deadly risks on every trip to carry food to his sister's family in Gütersloh. Eric's heart almost failed when he thought about all the secret stores of provisions that lay hidden in the barn under machinery, in the woodshed, or under piles of wood or rubbish about the place.

Added to these constant dangers, the radio with its short-wave band brought the London broadcast of foreign news into the parlor every night, and Father persisted in his habit of listening to it.

What if some inspector should find out the truth about the illegal activities in the *Gasthaus?* Eric dare not think of the consequences.

Father still sheltered Frau Stoll and her daughter in one of the upstairs guest rooms. Frau Schmidt and her son, Otto, grown more fanatical with every year of the war, kept sharp eyes open at all times. The refugees from both the eastern borders and the western could not be trusted. They were nearly crazed by hunger, grief, and terror. Children cried for no apparent reason. Older folk jerked at the most harmless sounds. The nerves of the whole population had been on edge for a long time.

Now, with Russian armies in the outskirts of Berlin and American troops on the Elbe, Father did not see how the final violence could be long delayed. He told the family his opinion and added, "Hitler has issued an order. I heard it a few days ago and I wrote it down:

> *Lay waste the country. . . .*
> *Destroy all food and clothing.*

Father looked around at them with a grave face. "This directive has not been carried out. No one has obeyed that mad man's orders. Hitler has lost his power over Germany."

Eric knew that another of Hitler's orders had not been enforced. On March 25 Hitler had commanded all the German people to gather in the central area of the Fatherland. What would they eat? Where would they sleep? What would they wear? Now Eric knew beyond any doubt that Father had spoken the truth—Hitler had gone mad!

The final break-up seemed close, and, anxious to prevent any additional violence and also to allay suspicion from any quarter, Father told Eric to take the two old guns, the swords, and the rifle and bury them in the orchard. Eric carried out

74

his Father's wish, but he felt sorry indeed to see the beautiful old weapons placed in their grave and felt as though some good friends had died.

One day in April a neighbor passed the *Gasthaus* and told Father that the Americans had reached Holtensen, a mile away.

Father went to his room and came back with a small American flag which he had kept hidden in an old trunk ever since he had come from America.

"Come, Eric." He handed him the flag. "We will go to meet them."

Eric hid the flag under his jacket, the same jacket that had kept him warm on those hideous nights of pig-butchering. He and Father got on their bicycles and rode into the crisp spring day.

Near Holtensen they saw tanks and knew that they must be American.

"Quick, Eric! Bring out the flag. Hold it high!"

For an instant Eric saw the soldiers hesitate. Then they recognized the Stars and Stripes and hurried forward. Father shook hands with them and talked to them in English. They gathered round him with smiles and kind greetings. They brought out chocolate bars and gave some to Eric. He unwrapped one and began eating it at once. He had not eaten chocolate for so long that he had forgotten how delicious it tasted.

He watched Father. He had never admired his Father so much. To Eric he had become a much greater hero than Adolf Hitler had ever been. The things Father had predicted had come true; while all the things Hitler had promised had failed—every one of them.

Now the Americans had come. Eric felt sure everything would be better at once. He nibbled on the second bar of chocolate and thought he had never felt more safe and content.

With more chocolate bars and many pleasant words, the soldiers said how glad they were to find a man from Michigan here in the center of Germany.

Father shook hands with them again. "Come over to my hotel, and we will find some good food for you and some good drinks too," he said.

The soldiers came that same day, and Father served them the best refreshments the Kreye family could furnish. These soldiers belonged to a tank brigade. They explained to Father that a tough job still lay ahead of them. The Nazis still held positions in many of the small villages dotted over the countryside. The tank brigade must search them out and convince them that Hitler's war had ended.

A short time after the soldiers left, a neighboring farmer stopped at the *Gasthaus*. He spoke to Father. "Did you see the Americans with tanks go along this road?"

"Yes, I did, just a short time ago."

"They were ambushed in Höfingen down the road a little way and a number of them are dead. One of them, the only survivor from his tank, is badly wounded, and he is calling for you—the man at the hotel who speaks English."

"Are you sure about this?" Father asked. Eric could see that Father could not believe that the young American soldiers who had set off laughing and joking not half an hour ago could now be dead and wounded.

"I'm sure he means you," the neighbor insisted. "He called you the man from Michigan."

Eric looked out the window and saw that people were bringing the wounded soldiers to a first-aid station just up the street half a block. Father ran out, and Eric followed him. He saw Father bend over a young soldier and heard him say, "Pray for me, Mr. Kreye. You are a good kind man."

Eric could not bear to go in where the young Americans

Eric and Father cautiously advanced as American
tanks came rumbling into the village.

were lying, some of them dying, he knew. He looked down and saw an army shoe thrown to one side, covered with blood and blasted with shrapnel. He picked up the shoe.

He stood there with the pitiful thing in his hand, and he thought of Hans. Had Hans died like the young soldier who had worn this shoe? A terrible ache filled his chest. He set the bloody shoe almost reverently by the door of the station and turned away.

Father did not come out for a long time. He explained that the American lad who had asked for him was nearly dead, but he had stayed to comfort the others. He could speak English.

eight

NOW FEELINGS RAN WILD and high. The conquerors felt an exuberance of victory; the conquered, the bitterness of defeat and loss. How could the loyal Hitler followers bear to see all their *Führer's* dreams of a mighty world empire dissolve in thunder, in rubble, and in blood? Many still persisted in fighting. Hitler had given his usual orders: "Victory or death!"

Whenever the soldiers could get liquor, they drank large quantities of it, and the results frightened everyone. One day drunken soldiers of the occupation forces came to the *Gasthaus* and demanded whiskey.

"There is no whiskey in this house," Father told them.

"You gave the German soldiers whiskey. Now give it to us!" One of them held a gun against Father's chest.

While this soldier continued to threaten Father with his gun, the other soldiers rampaged through the house, smashing doors, breaking windows, forcing open cupboards and tearing everything to pieces. When they failed to find whiskey they shouted again, "Whiskey! Whiskey! or we'll shoot you!"

Eric felt his blood trickle through his veins like icewater. He saw some of the soldiers rummaging through Mother's jewelry. She grabbed it out of their hands. Eric gasped. He had never seen Mother display such resistance, such courage. She defied the whole roomful of drunken soldiers.

"Come, there's nothing here," one of them who seemed to be their leader said. "Let's go."

They saw a basket of fresh eggs on the floor and grabbed it up. Others seized Father's bicycle and Eric's. They rode off, three on each bicycle, careening drunkenly down the street. They pelted one another with the eggs while their coarse laughter and blurred voices showed how much they enjoyed their little joke.

A short distance down the street they met an old gentleman, also riding a bicycle. They knocked him under the chin, and he fell backward to the pavement. They grabbed his bicycle. Now more of them could ride.

Eric had borne everything up to this point with stunned and heart-broken terror; but when he saw his own bicycle rolling off down the street with three drunken soldiers on it, he broke into hysterical sobbing which he could not control. He remembered how hard he had worked to earn the money for that bicycle. Even the thought—the certain knowledge— that thousands, even millions, of people in his own country had lost everything, had even been killed, could not stanch his tears. His own loss blinded him to what others had suffered.

Then, while they all stood watching, a jeep came roaring down the road loaded with high-ranking British officers. Father waved them to a halt and explained what had just happened. Then a truck load of other British soldiers came up. They stopped and heard the story. Then they all took out after the culprits and soon captured them. They even brought the bicycles back.

"Let's hide them in the attic." Father started to wheel his bicycle up the stairs. "We'll put them where they won't be so easy to pick up."

Eric followed, pushing his own bicycle and thinking how awful he'd felt a few minutes before and how glad and thankful he felt now.

"Those drunken wretches will be back," Father said. "When they come next time, they will be dangerous."

They shoved the two bicycles into an attic room and moved a heavy cabinet in front of the door. Father went all over the house tightening unbroken windows and locking doors. He finished his work not one minute too soon.

The first group of drunken rascals came back in a fury. They cut telephone wires, smashed more windows and tore up everything they could break apart. In the midst of the tumult Father vanished. Eric didn't know where he had gone. Had some of these drunken soldiers dragged him off and killed him? Anything was possible.

Again Mother faced the vandals with steadfast courage. Eric saw a black pistol in one soldier's hand. "Tell me where your man is." He threatened Mother with the pistol.

She pointed down the road and said in a calm voice, "You will find him in that direction."

The soldiers were too befuddled to question her directions or mistrust her tranquil self-possession. Some of them set off in the direction she had pointed. Others crashed through the house. They found the locked room of the refugee family upstairs and kicked in the door. The refugees burst out through the broken door like frightened rabbits and fled down the stairs and out into the street.

Eric saw the soldiers fire on the terrified refugees as they ran helter skelter toward the baker's house down the road, screaming at every leap.

Eric caught a glimpse of Irmgard through the window. She was running toward a neighbor's house. Now only Mother and he faced the drink-maddened soldiers.

He looked at Mother and knew they had both thought of the same thing. He caught Mother's hand and together they rushed out into the early darkness. He thought he heard Irmgard scream, but he couldn't be sure. Through the pastures they raced toward the creek.

The night settled down over them; but they knew the land well, and they thanked God for the protection the night gave them. The smell of fresh spring grass came up around them and the perfume of early flowers, but they did not slacken their pace until they reached Holtensen. They knew where the American troops were quartered.

They saw some soldiers around a fire. One of them called out to them. Then Mother went up to him and told him what had happened.

The sentry wakened his sleeping comrades, and in a few moments a battered army truck started toward Unsen. Along with Mother and Eric rode a goodly company of sober American soldiers.

They flashed their spotlights on both sides of the road, but the only unusual thing they saw was the old gentleman's bicycle with its frame twisted. It lay where it had been abandoned.

They found the *Gasthaus* quiet. The renegades had disappeared into the night. Eric thought of his own bicycle and ran to see if it had been taken again. He felt fortunate to find it safe where he and Father had put it.

Then he saw Father coming out of Frau Hölscher's room. He looked dusty, rumpled and disheveled. "She hid me behind the big corner clothespress," he explained trying to shake the cobwebs from his coat.

In that moment Eric forgave Frau Hölscher for all her meanness and petty thefts. She had saved Father's life.

Eric hurried to the basement to see what damage had been done there and found Ursula pale and trembling beside the milk-room door.

"What's the matter?" Eric almost panicked at seeing her look so frightened.

"One of them came down here looking for whiskey."

"Yes, I know. That's what they tore the house apart for— to find whiskey."

"Eric— I had a bottle of liquid soap— A brown bottle nearly full— I gave it to him."

"Then what?"

"He tipped back his head and took a long gulping drink— And then— He seemed to sober up— He ran out of here coughing and spitting bubbles like nothing you ever saw!"

Eric still trembled, but he couldn't help laughing. He laughed until tears choked him. "That must be why they left in such a hurry," he managed to say. "That's why they didn't do more damage. Oh, Ursula, I think that's great, just great! Too bad you couldn't have given them all a drink."

Ursula did not laugh. "But what if they come back?" He saw her lips tremble. "Next time they will kill us all."

But the drunken soldiers did not come back.

The April days crowded each other full of confusion and excitement. Then came the morning when Father announced to the family, "Hitler is dead!"

"How do you know?"

"I heard it over the London broadcast. He killed himself in Berlin on the twenty-first—one day after his fifty-fifth birthday."

No one spoke. No one moved. Eric thought of the two million people who had once rallied to cheer Adolf Hitler's birthday in Nürnberg. Now he had died by his own hand, and a Russian bomb had already obliterated his grave.

Then he thought of Hans, Hans who had loved Hitler so much, who had been willing and ready to go anywhere, even to die for Hitler. Hans must be dead too. The story they had heard must be true.

Eric had thought that when the Allied troops occupied Germany everything would be all right. He soon discovered how mistaken he had been. He began to understand that war is not only a terrible and a destructive thing while it rages, but war also leaves the countries who have fought each other with terrible wounds that cannot heal for many years—maybe never.

Father explained to him that the world would never be the same again. The millions of young soldiers who had fought on both sides and had been destroyed had robbed the future of all the children they might have had and all the useful work they might have done. This great crime, Father said, rested mostly on Adolf Hitler. History had never known such a scourge.

Food became even scarcer. Farmers had not been able to plow their land or to sow seed that spring, and now they faced an autumn without harvest. Refugees and displaced people roamed through the desolated land stealing everything they could find. The danger of starvation loomed larger now than during the war years. Hitler had escaped into a dishonored grave, but the fruits of his madness plagued his country with increasing severity.

One day, soon after Allied troops entered their valley, Eric saw a familiar figure at the *Gasthaus* door. "Hans!" He sprang forward to welcome his brother. "Oh, Hans! We thought you had been killed."

Mother came running from the kitchen and Father from

the barn. They enfolded the dear wanderer in such a warm welcome that Eric could see unshed tears glisten in the eyes of his disciplined Nazi brother.

He must sit up to the table. Mother must bring him something good to eat. Irmgard must hold onto his hand and gaze at him with adoring eyes, while Father said, in a husky voice, "Well, Son, tell us about it."

So Hans began his story:

"Of course you know that I went with the *Hitler-Jugend* to join the *Arbeitsdienst* near the Elbe. We prepared fortifications, dug trenches, and did other work like that." Hans began to eat the kuchen (sweet bread) Mother had brought with a glass of milk. "The Americans had reached our area. We knew that, but planes flew overhead all the time. We didn't pay too much attention to them. Then, one day when we were marching down the road, we saw some of the planes leave their formation, and we knew they meant to attack us. I suppose they thought we were a column of soldiers. The attack planes circled in. We broke ranks and scattered into the forest. They peppered the trees with bombs."

"What did you do Hans?" Irmgard looked at him with wondering eyes.

"Boys were being killed all around me. I ran."

"Where could you run?"

"Well, I decided right then that the best place to run would be toward the American lines." Hans hesitated. "I knew that the Allies had already won this war. Hitler had lost too many soldiers on the Russian front and on the western battlefields."

"Did they make you a prisoner?" Mother asked.

"Of course they did. But they had too much heavy fighting on their hands to take much notice of one boy who had given himself up. Later—quite a while later—the American officers called me in for questioning." A slow grin spread over Hans's

85

face. "You know what? When they found out I had been born in Michigan, they told me I was a United States citizen, and they let me go."

For a moment the whole family sat in stunned silence.

Hans looked at Eric. "You are an American citizen too. You were born in United States. Even though you left America when you were a small child, you are still a citizen."

Eric looked at Father, then at Mother. He couldn't believe what Hans had just told them.

"I'm sure Hans is correct," Father said. "I remember now that all persons born in United States are citizens by right of birth."

"Then will we go to America?" Eric asked.

"Nothing could please me more than to have my boys make their future in the United States." Father looked happier than Eric had seen him in years.

But going to United States proved to be a delayed and difficult matter for Eric and Hans. The farm must be cared for and restored to its pre-war production. The *Gasthaus* patronage, which had suffered much during the final years of the war, must be built again. The war years had impoverished the whole country, and the Kreye household felt the pinch along with all other German families.

nine

ONE DAY AN ORDER CAME for all persons who had been members of the *Gestapo* to come to Hameln to be registered and questioned. Father went, expecting to be back in a couple hours, but he did not return.

All through that December day the family waited for him. Then someone came to report that he had been detained by the occupation authorities.

"But why would they arrest Father? He never took Hitler's side." Eric watched Mother put on her warm things.

"Remember, the Nazis forced your father to become a member of the secret police, and three months passed before he could get away and come home again."

"I suppose they've found records."

"Of course, records were kept, you know," Mother started for Hameln to find out about Father.

When Mother came back, she told the family that Father had been imprisoned in the *Mittelschule* in Hameln, the same school Eric had attended. Now it had been made into a prison with barbed wire around it and guards on duty.

The next day Eric went with Mother to see Father. They were not allowed to enter the building. Father spoke to them from a third-floor window. He spoke cheerfully. "I have done nothing wrong. I'm sure I shall be out for Christmas. Tell Irmgard."

Eight days passed, but Father didn't come home.

All through the war Father had always cut the Christmas tree and decorated it for the children. He and Mother had never failed to make an enchanting surprise out of the holiday. Now the war had ended, and the most gloomy Christmas the children had ever known loomed ahead.

The days of Christmas week passed, one by one. Christmas Eve came and went, and still Father did not come. Then Mother found that Father had been transferred on Christmas Eve to a big camp at Ostsee, near Hamburg.

"What will they do with Father?" Eric couldn't help worrying.

"We can only wait and see. Your father is a good man, and he has done nothing wrong. We must hope and pray."

Irmgard missed Father so much that even the disappointment of Christmas did not seem to bother her. She asked all the time, "When will Father come?"

Eric found the wintertime chores heavy. Neither Ludwig nor Ursula worked on the Kreye farm anymore. Father had apprenticed Hans to a pharmacist in Bad Pyrmont, so he wasn't around to help either.

Then one day Father opened the *Gasthaus* door and walked in. He stood smiling at his family, and they rushed into his arms. Eric knew that nothing else mattered since Father had come home safe and well.

"Sorry I couldn't get here for Christmas," Father said.

"Oh, Father, having you home again is better than all the Christmases in the world." Irmgard snuggled into Father's arms although she had grown to be a big girl—twelve years old already.

Then Father told them about the pitiful condition of the soldiers in the prison camp. "I thought it must be run by the Russians. I asked to see the camp director at once, and within an hour I stood before him telling my story."

"What did you tell him?" Mother asked.

"I told him that because I spoke English, I had been forced to train for the Gestapo; but I had stayed only three months, and then I had been released and sent back to my farm." Then Father laughed, and Eric thought he had never heard a more pleasant sound. "You know what they did then? They assigned me to the 104th Tank Division—a new division they have just formed."

"Is it German?" Eric asked.

"Yes, of course. The German officers told me that if in the future anyone asks me where I spent the war, I must answer, 'In the 104th Tank Division.' "

"It is a joke then," Eric said.

"Well, I guess you might call it that. It's a convenience."

With Father home everything improved. Both Hans and Eric had applied for United States passports and planned to find their future in America. Hans had already entered his apprenticeship a few months before, but Eric still stayed on the farm and helped Father with the Gasthaus.

Eric had heard about the free and pleasant life in United States, the pleasure parties, the fairs and carnivals. He decided that if he expected to fit into the social activities of his new adventure he must learn to dance. He began to take lessons in Höfingen. He rode his bicycle to the dancing school which was conducted in an old building once or twice a week. About twenty-five couples danced to Strauss waltzes and other lively music.

89

Spring came, and Eric and Father finished the plowing and planting. Still the boys had not completed arrangements for their passage to America. They made several trips to Hamburg, but not until late in the fall could everything be cleared for their journey.

The last day at home finally came. Eric's suitcases were packed, and everything was ready for the trip the next day. The boys planned to go to Hamburg first and pay a farewell visit to the relatives there and then go on to Bremen.

A farewell party had been arranged by Hans's friends at the Wellhausen restaurant, the other public eating place in Unsen. Dances and parties were often held at the Wellhausen place. Volker was to be there, and most of both Hans's and Eric's young friends.

The party proved a great success, and Eric danced until after midnight. He had become quite clever at managing his feet; and he felt so confident, as a young man on his way to social success, that he took a drink of homemade schnapps (gin) which burned the whole length of his throat and made him cough and sputter in a somewhat undignified manner.

The following day Father and Mother stood on the station platform in Hameln waiting for the train that would carry the boys far away on a new venture into a new life in a far-off land.

"Remember, boys," Father said in a cheerful voice. "You will find a lot of Germany in the United States."

The train came. The boys said good-bye. Father and Mother seemed almost glad for them to go. Could it be because Germany was a destroyed country, while the United States had not been damaged?

The boys reached Hamburg late that afternoon and spent a short time with the relatives there. The destruction in the city seemed much worse than it had to Eric on his previous visit.

Two days later when the travelers arrived in Bremen, Eric

could hardly believe what his eyes saw. Many square miles of the city lay in ruins—a tangle of twisted wire, crushed brick, cracked concrete, and broken glass. They must stay in a camp out in the city suburbs to wait for their vessel to sail. The long ride out to the camp depressed Eric. The streetcar ran between acres of rubble on either side. This great seaport had suffered massive destruction from the terrible Allied bombing.

For two weeks they waited at the camp, and then came the day when they could board their ship, the S.S. *Ernie Pyle,* a converted troop transport. As they stood with their few pieces of baggage waiting for it to be carried aboard, a friendly gentleman approached them. "Are you boys going to New York?"

"Yes we are," Hans answered.

"You have only a few pieces of luggage. I wonder if you would be so kind as to take a couple of my suitcases on your tickets."

Hans and Eric looked at each other. "I think we could do that, sir," Hans said.

The man brought two large suitcases and changed the tags on them so they could go with Hans and Eric's luggage. They saw the things safely stored in the hold and found their stateroom. Then they went on deck to see the ship slip its cables. As the distance widened between the *Ernie Pyle* and the shore, Eric suddenly realized how great a distance he was putting between himself and his home, Father, Mother, Irmgard, and the green valley of his childhood.

Then another thought swept through his mind; he knew that this ship would carry him far from the land ruined, devastated, scourged by eight years of Adolf Hitler's mad thrust for power. The date on the calendar was Tuesday, November 19, 1947.

Eleven days after leaving Bremen the *Ernie Pyle* steamed

into calm waters. The rolling, pitching, corkscrewing motions which had distressed Eric so much quieted. Flocks of sea-gulls flew over the ship. "We shall set our feet on land tomorrow," one of the passengers said.

The man's words struck Eric with a strange sensation. Tomorrow he would stand on the soil of his own country—the land of his birth. Yet, to him, the United States seemed a vast foreign nation. He knew that if people could look into his heart and mind they would find the name of Germany written there, although his passport carried the official seal of the United States of America.

Then he remembered Father's parting words, "You will find much of Germany in the United States." He wondered now if he had understood what Father meant.

"All luggage must be on deck by seven o'clock tomorrow morning," one of the ship's officers announced through a loudspeaker.

Hans and Eric packed all their things that evening and then went on deck to see how New York harbor looked at night. Moonlight glistened on the water, and Eric could see the shoreline beaded with lights. "Oh, look, Hans, the lights are moving. There must be thousands of them."

"Automobiles, I think." Hans studied the lights.

"I never dreamed there could be so many automobiles in all the world."

That night Eric could sleep little for thinking of all the exciting events rushing together for tomorrow. His mind anticipated all manner of pleasant surprises.

The boys ate breakfast that Saturday morning at six o'clock, and they carried their hand baggage up to the deck before seven.

Eric looked out at a typical harbor scene. The *Ernie Pyle* drew slowly in among many other ships of all sizes and flying the flags of many nations—freighters, passenger vessels, tugs, barges, tankers, and every other kind of craft large and small. Little boats darted through the water plying between ships and piers. Excitement rode the air like an invisible wave.

Then Eric saw the fireboats. They shot streams of water high into the air. They seemed to be saluting one of the big liners that slowly moved in among them. The monster vessel acknowledged the display of water with low whistles. Eric tried to count the fireboats, but he couldn't. There seemed to be quite a few, and the streams of water they shot into the air soared as high as a forest tree and broke into tumbling spray —quite a show! Eric had never heard of such a thing.

"Look! The Statue of Liberty!" someone cried out.

The boys looked out and saw the giant figure straight ahead. "I wish we could have seen it last night. It's lighted at night, isn't it?" some person near the boys exclaimed.

Eric could see the torch in the statue's hand and made up his mind that one day he would visit that statue and climb the stairs that someone had told him wound up to the top of the tall figure. It would be like climbing the *Süntelturm* back in his home valley.

Again a booming voice announced, "United States citizens will be permitted to land first."

Eric and Hans looked at each other. Queer, yes almost impossible, to think of themselves as United States citizens.

But they did not leave the ship with the first passengers ashore. The friendly gentleman whose baggage they had accepted in Bremen was not an American citizen, and they must wait until he cleared customs. Hour after hour went by, and Eric felt that he could not endure the delay. Surely someone had come to meet them—maybe Uncle Arthur and Aunt Charlotte Jellinghaus, or maybe Great Aunt Wittig. Now surely the United States relatives would think they hadn't come. What if he and Hans should be turned loose in the great city of New York without knowing how to speak English. They hadn't any money either. They hadn't needed any on board the ship but now—

After five hours the gentleman finally cleared customs and claimed his two suitcases with a grunt of acknowledgment, nothing more.

Then the boys rushed out to see if any friendly person waited to offer them welcome to this huge and noisy land.

Great Aunt Wittig came forward and greeted them with such an affectionate welcome that they forgot their anxiety in the wonder of being at last in the United States. Aunt Wittig hired a taxi, and they drove through canyon-like streets crowded with people on foot and more people in innumerable automobiles. She answered all their questions in German. She called their attention to men who were fastening up Christmas decorations all along the street.

Eric could not help comparing this huge city of New York with Hamburg and Bremen. No bombs had fallen here. Every office building, every factory, every church and home stood undamaged. What a blockbuster could do dropped into the center of this street! Eric shuddered.

The taxi took them to Grand Central Station. They entered the enormous vaulted building, and Eric could see Christmas decorations all about him. He heard the strains of organ music —"Jesu, Joy of Man's Desiring." The glorious strains echoed throughout the vast structure. Aunt Wittig must have made a mistake and brought them to a cathedral of some sort. Father had been right about finding Germany in the United States— Bach's music in the first building they walked into.

Then Aunt Wittig led the boys to the ticket counter, and Eric saw that this huge and majestic building must indeed be a railway station. She bought them tickets to Syracuse, New

94

The boys noticed a giant figure ahead of the ship.
Then someone shouted, "The Statue of Liberty!"

York, and put a bag of lunch into each boy's hand. Then she led them to a place where huge engines roared in and out, pulling their trains of passenger coaches. "Now, you just stay right on this train, and Uncle Arthur and Aunt Charlotte will meet you in Syracuse." Aunt Wittig waved good-bye until the train carried them out of the station.

The boys found comfortable seats and looked about them. The coach seemed uncrowded—such a contrast to the trains between Hameln and Hamburg. They looked out their window and decided that the winter landscape flowing past looked much like the German countryside.

Then they opened their lunch bags. Eric thought that since they had eaten breakfast many hours ago, maybe the time had come to taste food in the United States. They found delicious sandwiches, bananas, oranges, and the biggest candy bars they had ever seen. Eric began on a candy bar at once and finished it as fast as he could, scarcely stopping to catch his breath.

All the rest of the day they spent on the train watching the snowy farms and winter woods and villages speed past. Sometimes they dozed a little. Dark night had fallen when their train pulled into Syracuse.

ten

AT THE STATION IN SYRACUSE Uncle Arthur and Aunt Charlotte waited for the boys. Eric had seen many pictures of this Uncle and Aunt, and he recognized them at once. They greeted the boys with warm affection, loaded their suitcases into their car, drove through Syracuse and continued another hour on to Pulaski and the Jellinghaus farm. Light snow fell all the way, and when they reached the farm they found it covered with a thick, soft blanket of white.

"Well, boys," Uncle Arthur said as they took off their coats and mittens in the warm kitchen, "we have thirty acres of excellent farm land here. We have pasture for our cows. We have hay land and woods and enough room for a good garden. We keep bees too."

After giving the boys a good supper, Aunt Charlotte put them in snug beds where they soon dropped into slumber.

At breakfast the next morning Eric noticed that Uncle Arthur had on his work clothes. Aunt Charlotte didn't seem to be dressed up either, yet he knew that it must be Sunday. Or could he have been mistaken?

97

"What work can you do on the farm in winter?" Hans asked.

"We haul manure to fertilize the ground for the coming year's crops. Then there is always milking to do morning and evening." Uncle Arthur smiled his slow, kind smile. "I think you boys will find it much like home. I hope so."

Eric looked at the good breakfast Aunt Charlotte had set before them—delicious canned fruit, fresh cream and butter with home-baked bread—and judged that this house would seem much like home. He noticed that Aunt Charlotte had put a fancy glass dish full of chocolate candies on the living-room table. These, he had to admit, were not like home. For many years there had been no chocolate candy in Unsen. Yet he approved. Oh, yes, he approved with an enthusiasm he hoped he could control!

"You want to run the tractor, Eric?" Uncle Arthur said after they had finished breakfast.

"Of course!" Eric jumped to his feet.

"No," Uncle Arthur raised his hand. "Just wait until we read our Morning Watch." He picked up a little book that lay beside his plate. After he had read a few paragraphs and offered a short prayer, Uncle Arthur said, "All right, Eric, here we go."

Eric pulled on his warm clothing. He'd seen pictures of that tractor before he left Germany, and he'd dreamed for months of getting his hands on that wheel. Now he'd learn to drive it.

But the day didn't seem like Sunday. He sensed something queer and different about his Uncle's home. And what could that book be that Uncle had read from that morning? He'd called it "Morning Watch." What kind of book could that be?

He helped Uncle Arthur load manure; then they pulled it with the tractor and spread it over the snow on the garden.

Uncle let Eric drive the tractor back to the barn. His heart swelled with such pride that he scarcely felt the nipping cold. Imagine! He could control this big machine.

That evening Uncle Arthur introduced both boys to the cows and the milking machine. Eric thought he had never seen such an astonishing thing. The cows didn't seem to mind having a machine milk them. They appeared to enjoy it. Eric and Hans helped Uncle carry the pails of milk into the milk room.

After supper that night the boys went upstairs to their comfortable room, and Eric recalled that nothing had been said about Sunday evening church service. Could he have gotten mixed up about the days in all the excitement of their first hours in United States? He thought about asking Hans, but Hans had already fallen asleep.

Then Eric heard the sound of voices from his Uncle and Aunt's room downstairs and directly below where he lay. He knew their bedroom door at the foot of the stairs stood open and a register in the floor let the warm air come up into the bedroom where he was. He listened again. Now he could hear just one voice. Uncle Arthur seemed to be reading to Aunt Charlotte.

He raised himself on his elbow and recognized the book that Uncle was reading—the Bible. He heard the reading end, and then both their voices came up to him distinctly. They must be praying. He heard them mention his name and Hans's. He lay back on his pillow satisfied that Uncle Arthur and Aunt Charlotte still loved and worshiped God. He must have been mistaken about the day. Tomorrow must be Sunday.

Next morning at breakfast Eric asked his aunt, "Is today Sunday?"

"No, Eric, yesterday was Sunday."

Eric paused with his spoonful of applesauce halfway to his mouth and looked at her.

She laughed, "Oh, Eric, I know what you are thinking. Yes, Uncle Arthur and I do go to church, but we go on the Sabbath. We are Seventh-day Adventists."

"Are they Christians?"

"Yes, they are Christians who follow Christ's example. He kept the Sabbath—the seventh day of the week." Aunt Charlotte brought the glass candy dish from the living room and refilled it.

Eric thought about what Aunt Charlotte had said while he finished breakfast. Then Uncle Arthur took the same little book from beside his plate. "This is our Morning Watch book, boys. It has a Bible text for each day of the year and a few words of comment and explanation." Then, just as he had done the day before, he prayed a short prayer before the family went about their morning tasks.

One evening as the boys prepared for bed, Eric said, "I don't understand Uncle Arthur and Aunt Charlotte's religion, but they seem to be quite enthusiastic about it."

"I can't stand all this praying and Bible reading," Hans said. "I'm going to find a place where I can continue my training as a pharmacist. I think I'll write to Uncle George in Michigan."

"But Hans," Eric said, "they pray only at breakfasttime. They have evening prayer in their own bedroom."

"Yes, I know they do," Hans looked annoyed. "I know they do. They pray for us. I've heard them. Well, I don't like that any better than prayers at breakfasttime."

"They don't try to influence us or force us to believe like they do." Eric wondered why Hans felt so defensive about it.

"Just the same it makes me uncomfortable." Hans burrowed under the covers, and Eric found himself, as he did so often, alone with his own thoughts.

Eric felt at home with Uncle Arthur and Aunt Charlotte. The gentle warmth that filled their farmhouse came not from the heating system alone, though the furnace in the basement seemed adequate. Eric had seen the big asbestos-covered pipes that carried heat to the different rooms. No, the warmth he felt came from the kind hearts of the two people who lived in this home.

Winter continued cold and blustery. Uncle Arthur worked five days a week at his trade of electrician. He must drive the thirty-six miles to his shop in Syracuse every morning and return at night. Eric could see that having a couple of husky farm boys around the place made Uncle's work easier.

Many mornings Eric and Hans wakened early and shoveled a path to the highway so Uncle could get his car out. Although the driveway didn't look long, it seemed like a great distance when it had to be shoveled clear of the deep and heavy snow. For many days the temperature stayed below zero.

Before many weeks Hans got in touch with Uncle George in Michigan and left to continue his pharmaceutical training in Grand Rapids.

Eric stayed on with Uncle Arthur and Aunt Charlotte. Now he began to attend church with them. The first Sabbath he understood only one word of the sermon—Peter! The sincerity and devotion of the speaker, however, showed through his voice and the kind look on his face. Eric went again and again and began to understand more words.

Now he listened to his Uncle's favorite radio program—the *Voice of Prophecy*. He couldn't understand the words, but again the spiritual quality of the speaker's voice he could feel and enjoy with heart and mind. He loved the beautiful music. When he discovered that he could enroll for a course of Bible lessons in the German language, he sent in his name at once.

Then Aunt Charlotte gave him a Bible. Never before had he

101

owned a Bible, and now he could read this one with no trouble at all. It spoke his own language—German.

One evening at supper Uncle Arthur spoke to him. "Eric, spring will soon be here. I want you to have a good opportunity to work and earn money this spring and summer."

"But I like it here, Uncle Arthur, and you need me more than ever now that spring is coming."

"Yes, Eric, that is all true, and you are good help; but I wrote to a friend of mine who is a beekeeper in Wisconsin. Now I have received a letter from him." Uncle pulled an envelope from his pocket. "Mr. Kruse writes that he will be glad to give you a job."

Sharp and stinging experiences during his childhood had taught Eric something about bees. He didn't feel at all sure that he would enjoy being a beekeeper. Still the job looked like an opportunity to learn more about his new country, the United States. Also it offered the challenge of a new skill which he might learn.

In April, 1948, Eric said good-bye to Uncle Arthur and Aunt Charlotte. He found it hard to leave them, for they had treated him like a favorite son. He had not been too lonesome for home, because his uncle's home felt so much like his father's house. He had come to respect the religion there, and he had learned a little English.

eleven

IN REEDSBURG, WISCONSIN, Eric found his uncle's friend waiting for him with a hearty welcome. Mr. Kruse loaded Eric's baggage into the panel truck that he used to deliver honey. It even smelled like beeswax and honey.

On the way from the station to the Kruse home in Loganville, Eric thought to himself that perhaps he would soon be driving this truck. Instead of hauling manure with a tractor he would deliver a much sweeter load—honey.

Eric found Mr. Kruse, his new employer, a quick, energetic, and generous man. "I don't want you to work in the beeyards too soon," he said. "If too many bees sting you right away, you will get discouraged."

He put Eric to work in his shop with two other boys. They built new hives and repaired old ones. They constructed frames on which the bees would deposit honey. Later Eric learned to work with the bees—two thousand hives of them. He came to like his work and his employer.

Wisconsin with its rolling hills and waving grainfields, its orchards and gardens, reminded him of Unsen and the Süntel.

Mr. Kruse followed the same religion that Uncle Arthur and Aunt Charlotte valued so much. He took Eric to church with him and often included him in what he called his "missionary work." He handed out tracts and magazines to people and told them about the Adventist belief, which he seemed to regard as the most precious thing in the world.

Now Eric began to wonder about the Sabbath. From reading his *Voice of Prophecy* lessons, he could see that God had commanded men to observe the seventh day of the week as the Sabbath. Yet his thoughts troubled him. Father and Mother had always been Christians. Nobody could convince him otherwise, yet they kept Sunday.

That summer Mr. Kruse took Eric on a short trip to Florida where he had fifteen hundred hives of bees near Homestead. They found plenty of work waiting for them. They cleaned the beeyards and put them in neat shape. Later in the fall the Florida caretaker would harvest the delicious orange-flower honey. Eric had tasted it and understood why it sold so well.

Back in Wisconsin the summer's work kept both of them busy. Eric had begun to like the job of beekeeper.

One day while Eric worked with Mr. Kruse in the beeyard, his employer said, "Eric, I think you ought to go back to school. I would like to send you to one of our academies, and I will help with your expenses."

Eric felt as though someone had doused him with a bucket of icewater. "Me? Me, go back to school? Never!"

Mr. Kruse didn't say any more that day, but Eric couldn't get the words out of his mind. For the next few days he tried to shut from his thoughts the challenging questions Mr. Kruse's suggestion had raised.

What did he intend to do with his life? How much actual schooling had he gotten in Germany during the war years? Would it be adequate for a man's lifework?

104

In spite of his attempt to stifle them, these questions and others kept rising up before him as though some other part of himself stood up and argued with him.

"Your school study in Germany didn't amount to much. The bombings disturbed it too often," the inner voice said.

Yes, Eric must admit that he hadn't studied a great deal.

"You are making a new life in a new country. Better learn all you can, you'll need it."

Eric admitted the truth of this argument too.

"God has important work for you to do. Shouldn't you prepare yourself?"

Eric bristled at this suggestion. Where could it be coming from? Must be that he'd listened too much to Uncle Arthur and Aunt Charlotte's religion. He'd gone to the Seventh-day Adventist church too, and then this spring and summer with Mr. Kruse had got him to thinking like an Adventist. But he wasn't an Adventist. He'd been baptized as a baby, and confirmed during the war years, in the old Lutheran Church in Holtensen. Sure, he'd been a Christian all his life, but what could all this conflict have to do with going back to school?

Through the days that followed, as Eric helped Mr. Kruse wind up his summer work with the bees, the older man brought up the subject of school again and again.

"We have a fine institution in Bethel Academy here in Wisconsin. I'm sure you would enjoy being there."

Eric didn't answer, "Never!" as he had the first time Mr. Kruse mentioned school; but his mind began to grapple with a great problem, and he spent many serious hours in thought.

All his life he had been pushed by circumstances. He had gone through the war years in Germany in the Hitler *Jungvolk,* and later the *Hitler-Jugend,* where he had followed orders. He had seen Hitler rise to power and go down to a dishonored grave dragging a ruined country with him. Eric realized that up to now he had never made a strong decision for himself. Never before had he stood up and chosen a course of action with deliberate intention. Now he felt himself being dragged into a personal conflict for which he had no weapons.

He knew that the Bible taught Sabbath keeping. He knew that not one text could be found to support Sunday observance. Yet his mind always went back to Father and Mother. Their dear kind faces rose before his mind, and he remembered so many things that convinced him that they were true Christians. Yet they kept Sunday as a holy day. Could such good and dedicated people be mistaken?

For days he thought about these things, and his mind became more and more troubled. He knew that Bethel Academy must be a Seventh-day Adventist school. If he should go there, wouldn't it be some kind of commitment?

One day Mr. Kruse laid a letter by his plate at lunchtime. "An application blank from Bethel Academy," he explained. "Look it over. Maybe you will decide to fill it out."

Eric pulled the paper from the envelope and unfolded it. A series of questions caught his eye:

Have you ever used tobacco? . . . Liquor?

Have you ever attended motion picture shows? . . . Theaters? . . . Dances?

Have you played cards?

Eric would have to answer "yes" to all those questions. Would Bethel Academy reject his application because of that? Of course he hadn't done any of these things while he lived with Uncle Arthur and Aunt Charlotte or later when he came to work for Mr. Kruse.

Do you use profane language?

He could mark a big black "no" for that one. Mother had taught him never to use profane or vulgar expressions.

Are you desirous of being a Christian—of living a Christian life?

This question struck at the heart of the problem he had wrestled with for days. Living a Christian life meant letting Jesus live in his heart and mind and letting Jesus direct his actions. Living a Christian life meant keeping God's holy law, and the Sabbath commandment stood in the center of that law.

Eric picked up the envelope and the application blank and started for his room.

"Don't worry about clothes or entrance fees. I'll see that you have the proper things to begin school." Mr. Kruse called after him.

"Thank you. I must give serious thought to this matter." Eric went into his room and shut the door. He knew that Mr. Kruse must have seen the worried look on his face and supposed that financial problems troubled him.

He drew out the Bible his Aunt Charlotte had given him and the unfinished packet of *Voice of Prophecy* lessons. He looked to see what lesson he had sent in last—one about the Sabbath. And the next one? Another lesson about the Sabbath!

Strange that a day of the week could raise such a disturbance in his mind. He tried to calm himself and think the matter through. He had read the Genesis story and knew that God had named the days of the week at Creation; first day, second day, third day, and so on. No one could doubt that God had established the seven-day week, or that he had set apart the seventh day as a holy rest day.

Eric opened his Bible and turned to the fourth commandment:

Remember the Sabbath day, to keep it holy. Six days shalt thou labor, and do all thy work: but the seventh day is the Sabbath of the Lord thy God: in it thou shalt not

107

do any work, thou, nor thy son, nor thy daughter, thy manservant, nor thy maidservant, nor thy cattle, nor thy stranger that is within thy gates: for in six days the Lord made heaven and earth, the sea, and all that in them is, and rested the seventh day: wherefore the Lord blessed the Sabbath day, and hallowed it. Exodus 20:8-11.

He closed his Bible, took out the application blank for Bethel Academy. He answered all the questions and signed him name. The next morning he mailed the letter. He had decided that if the academy would accept him, he would go.

Mr. Kruse seemed delighted over Eric's decision. "Now, don't worry about anything. All of us will help you. The registration comes soon now."

And they did help him. Mr. Kruse and the church people furnished him with clothing and bedding. Eric had grown taller and heavier since he had come to Uncle Arthur's house almost ten months before. None of his clothes from Germany fit him anymore.

Eric saw the things being readied for him, and he couldn't understand why Mr. Kruse could be so sure that the academy would accept him. But in a few days the acceptance came, and Mr. Kruse loaded Eric and his belongings into the honey truck and took him over to the academy.

Eric thought to himself, "It should be easy for me to be a good Christian at this school—no smoking, no drinking, no dancing, no bad language. These young people must be the cream of the country."

He liked the schoolgrounds. Although the buildings looked old and shabby, the lawns around them spread a green plush carpet, and the trees and meadows reminded him of Unsen.

The farm manager assigned Eric work in the barn, and he felt at home there. He helped care for the cows and did other chores. In the classroom he did not feel at home. He felt awkward. He understood and spoke little English. At Uncle Arthur's home it hadn't mattered about English. They all talked German. Later with Mr. Kruse he had spoken German too. The letters he received from Germany every week and the ones he wrote home were all in German. He had to face it. His knowledge of English amounted to almost nothing.

He studied long hours and applied himself with all the energy of his new decision to prepare himself for a successful future. The first semester's grades were a disappointment.

Other things began to trouble him too. Sometimes on going into the other boys' rooms he smelled tobacco smoke. A few times he saw a playing card dropped on the floor and knew that a card game must have ended suddenly when he knocked on the door. Hadn't these boys filled out the same application blank he had? Weren't they trying to be Christians? He knew that some of them belonged to the seminar and were planning to become preachers. Eric couldn't figure it out.

One evening he came upstairs after work and saw a big garbage can standing in the hallway right at the top of the stairs. Two boys carried buckets of water from the bathroom and filled it.

"What are you going to do with that?" he asked.

"Wait and see," one of the boys chuckled. "We're going to have some great fun with all this water."

Eric saw the boys tip the full garbage can down the stairs. The water made a tremendous splash. Most of it rushed into the dean's room at the foot of the stairs. Eric could imagine what that water did to the dean's carpet.

He went into his room and shut the door. So this is a Christian school, he thought. Father had always taught him to respect other people's property. This school had been dedi-

109

cated to God. The teachers were always reminding the students that this was a dedicated place. How dare those boys damage the Lord's property? He felt more discouraged than ever. Why should he stay at this academy any longer? That night he made up his mind to leave school.

twelve

ERIC HAD MADE UP HIS MIND to leave Bethel Academy, but a few days must pass before he could make arrangements for a job. Meanwhile he kept on attending classes.

The next day in Bible class his teacher, Elder Anderson looked at him with special attention. "Is something troubling you, Eric?" He did not wait for an answer. "Come to my office after classes are over for today."

All through the rest of the morning Eric wondered what Elder Anderson would say to him. How had Elder Anderson been able to read his troubled mind, and why should he care?

When at last he stood before his teacher's desk, he could think of nothing to say. The matter had been settled in his mind. By this time next week he'd be far from this discouraging place.

"What did you come to school for, Eric?" the teacher asked him. "Why did you come to Bethel Academy?"

Eric tried to collect his confused thoughts. "I wanted to learn more." He felt sure of that. "I wanted to live a Christian life."

"Sit down in that chair, Eric. Let's talk this matter over."
Elder Anderson sat down too. "You have found both these
goals difficult to reach? Is that not so?"

Eric squirmed a little. "English is a hard language to learn,
and I don't do well at it. My grades are not good."

"That problem will clear up. You will find your lessons
easier as time passes and you learn the language better." The
teacher seemed to be probing Eric with his eyes. "Now
the second problem: You do believe in the Lord Jesus Christ?"

"Yes, from my childhood my parents taught me to pray to
Jesus and to follow His teachings."

Elder Anderson leaned forward and spoke in an earnest tone
of voice. "Can it be, Eric, that you find it difficult to live a
Christian life here at Bethel Academy because you are looking
to people instead of to Jesus?"

Eric moved uneasily in his chair, but he said nothing.

"There will always be people who claim to be Christians
but are hypocrites. We are told not to follow men or walk
after their ways. We must follow Jesus and never take our
eyes or our faith from Him.

"But—but—"

"Let me tell you a little story, Eric. Maybe it will help you
to understand your problem. One day a group of people
accompanied their new missionary up a steep mountainside
on the island of Sumatra. The narrow path was bordered on
both sides by tall lallang grass. When the travelers came to
the steepest part of the climb, they reached out to take hold of
the grass to pull themselves up. Everyone in the line shouted
'Grasp it firmly! Grasp it firmly!' So the missionary grabbed
a handful of the tough, coarse grass and held it. Then he
grabbed another handful and another until they reached the
top.

"Then the missionary asked his companions why they had all

112

shouted, 'Grasp it firmly!' They told him that if any person takes hold of the lallang grass lightly or fearfully, the razor-sharp edges will cut his hands and make deep and painful wounds."

Eric thought for a long time while his teacher sat waiting. "You think, then, that I have not taken a firm hold on the Christian life?"

"You will have to judge that matter, Eric. I have found that many young Christians get hurts and discouragements because they have not taken a firm and determined stand for Christ." He stood up, and his voice was soft and gentle. "You see, my boy, the Christian life is a war against evil. We must take our stand under the flag we mean to defend, and we must grasp our weapons and step out with courage. Our Leader goes before us. We follow the blood-stained banner of our crucified Lord."

After Eric and Elder Anderson had prayed together, Eric walked back to his dormitory. His mind flashed back to the oath he had taken in the Hitler *Jungvolk*. He had promised to follow the "Blood Banner" of his *Führer* even to death.

He questioned himself. "Does Jesus Christ deserve as determined and faithful followers?" Now he could see it all plainly. Hitler had set himself up as a leader, but he had been only a frail and wicked human being. Now another Leader commanded him to follow, to pledge his life and obedience.

Eric determined to take his stand under the "Blood Banner" of Jesus Christ. He would not look to his schoolmates but would grasp the Christian way of life with both hands and keep his eyes on his Leader.

So Eric enlisted in the army of King Jesus. He realized at last that a man cannot go through life without taking a firm stand on something. Otherwise he must slide down into defeat and ruin.

8—U.B.B.

With Eric's new decision came a new kind of experience. He found more evidence of God's watching over him with constant care. He knew more moments of time when he sensed God's presence. He began to discover that a Christian experience is an active and satisfying series of events.

One day Eric and some of his friends stood behind a closed window watching some workmen use dynamite to blast holes for a power line. Without any reason, he ducked his head just as a two-by-four shattered the window and sailed through exactly where his head had been seconds before.

"Why did you duck?" one of his friends asked him when the boys had recovered a little from their shock.

Eric put his hand to his head. "I don't know. I just don't know. Something must have pushed me down!" Had an invisible hand pushed him down? Had an inaudible voice warned him? Eric could come to only one conclusion—God had saved his life!

Faith grew in him. He had determined to grasp the truth and hold it firmly. God had answered that faith with a sense of the divine Presence and a protective care that Eric could see and feel more every day.

During the second semester Eric found his schoolwork becoming less difficult. He began to understand English and to speak it with more freedom.

Then came the spring Week of Prayer, and a number of students at Bethel Academy made the decision to surrender their lives to God's will and service. Without hesitation Eric joined the group. A baptism was planned in the Yellow River.

As Eric stood with the others on the riverbank, he thought no springtime had ever seemed so lovely, no trees such a tender green, no skies so blue, no river so symbolic of the river of God which flowed through Eden. As he rose from the water, his heart overflowed with love for every living thing. Every

114

beautiful manifestation of God's love thrilled his heart and mind.

Back at his room in the dormitory he sat down to write letters to the dear ones in Germany. First he must write to Father and Mother. Not for a moment did he doubt their joy in his new experience. Hadn't they set his feet in the path that had led at last to his present dedication and his baptism?

School closed, and he took up his summer's work. He wanted to have as much money as possible on hand when school should open in the fall. Now, with his new grasp of English he had hopes of finishing the academy in three years instead of the usual four. He discovered that he had learned quite a lot in Germany after all.

He went back to Loganville to spend the summer working with Mr. Kruse's bees. Before he had been a week at Mr. Kruse's house, the answers began to come from his letters sharing his faith with his family. Many of his relatives and friends disapproved of what he had done. They accused him of forsaking the faith of his fathers and denying the commitment of his childhood.

Had his letter been that hard to understand? He had not forsaken the faith of his fathers. Hadn't he made that plain? He had gone forward into a new dimension, a larger room, a clearer vision, a real dedication to a real Leader, the Lord Jesus. Before, he had been tossed about on waves of uncertainty. Now, he knew himself anchored in the love of God and His truth.

Most distressing of all was Father's letter. Eric could only spread it out before the Lord while he knelt in tears and perplexity beside it.

Then he carried it to his friend, Mr. Kruse. "I have broken my father's heart." Eric explained in a faltering voice. "He is a good man, a devoted Christian gentleman. He loves me. He taught me from my earliest childhood to love and obey God. What shall I do?"

With patient care they read the letter again and again trying to understand the feeling that lay behind each word.

"I can see that your father is an honest and a dedicated man," Mr. Kruse said at last. "To him, it looks as if you have abandoned the faith of your childhood, your family, and your country."

"But I haven't." Eric folded the letter and put it back in the envelope. "I have not departed from my Father's teachings. He has said many times, 'God's law is above man's law. We ought to obey God rather than man.'"

"You must remember that it will take time for your parents to understand why you have chosen to keep the seventh-day Sabbath and be baptized by immersion."

"But both these doctrines are part of Christ's example and teaching."

"Eric, only love and tenderness and the gentle work of the Holy Spirit can bring together hearts that have been torn apart by religious differences. Begin now to build a bridge of prayer, of affection and patience. God grant your father will use the same materials to build his bridge toward you. I am sure he loves you as only a Christian father can love his son."

Comforted, Eric went back to his work. He knew that nothing could shake his determination to follow Christ all the way, to hold fast to truth and endure to the end. But the long silences where once there had been loving communication, the empty mailbox when letters from Germany had been his constant pleasure and comfort—these saddened Eric, and he realized that it is through much tribulation that we enter into the kingdom of heaven.

Eric returned to the academy, and the school years passed,

two more of them. During the summers Eric now worked for Mr. Ahlers. Brother and Sister Ahlers called him their adopted son and often invited him to their house for Sabbath dinner. Their house reminded him of home—the spotless rooms, the well-behaved children, and the warm family atmosphere comforted him. But he couldn't stay with the Ahlerses. He must live in the dormitory.

English at last came naturally to his tongue. He began to think in English. When the third and last year of Eric's stay at the academy drew toward its close the senior class organized and chose him as class pastor.

"What a change!" Eric thought. "When I came to this school three years ago last fall I had to put on my application blank that I smoked, drank, danced, and played cards. Now they have made me class pastor!"

The class adopted as their motto, "Simplicity, Sincerity, Service." Their aim, "To Build for Eternity." Their special Bible text, "In all thy ways acknowledge Him, and He shall direct thy paths." Proverbs 3:6.

Graduation week came at last. Eric stood in the chapel decorated in the class colors, green and gold. Great bouquets of yellow roses, the class flower, stood along the front of the platform. He went forward to get his diploma. He stood in line with the other graduates to greet all the people who offered their congratulations.

Then Eric went to his room, took off his cap and gown, folded them neatly, and sat down on the edge of his bed to think.

He picked up a letter which had just come from Germany. Irmgard would be coming to United States soon. He must meet her in New York. His heart warmed at the thought of seeing his little sister again. She had been so young when he left Germany—must be a woman now.

He looked again at the last sentence in Father's letter. He had read it many times. "I am very proud of you, my son." The bridge between them had been built again just as Mr. Kruse had hoped.

Eric had made plans to attend Emmanuel Missionary College that fall, and he would work for Mr. Ahlers during the summer. The Ahlerses had furnished the money to bring Irmgard to the United States. These kind people had become like parents to him.

He stood this day at an important milestone of his life, but he knew that the direction of his march had been set when he made his decision to grasp the Christian life with both hands, firmly. He had taken the weapons of his warfare in hand, enlisted under the Blood Banner of the Prince of Peace. He knew that certain victory lay ahead. With a thankful heart he stepped out into the spring afternoon.

Epilogue

All the events of this story happened a good many years ago. Eric Kreye now serves as staff artist at the Pacific Press Publishing Association in Mountain View, California, where he lives with his wife, Arbie, and their two daughters, Nancy and Linda. One of his favorite tasks, because it is of such importance to youth, is assisting in the preparation of *Listen* magazine. The boy who once smoked and who dispensed drinks in his father's *Gasthaus* now takes his greatest pleasure in being one of the artists for a leading temperance journal.

Irmgard did come to America. She also accepted the truth as Jesus taught and lived it. She became the wife of a missionary to Africa.

Hans is now a successful pharmacist in Michigan.

Frevie lost his life in the Foreign Legion.

Volker is now mayor of Unsen.

Eric has just returned from a visit to his parents in Germany. Once more he climbed the 108 steps to the crown of the *Süntelturm* and looked out over the lovely valley where he spent his boyhood years. With a heart overflowing with joy and thankfulness, he had no need to shout "Heil Hitler!" The words on his lips were, "Praise God!"

Since returning to America Eric has received this letter from his father:

> *The fact of your being an Adventist doesn't upset me anymore. I am proud to have such a Christian son.*
>
> *You are a good boy, and you want only the best for your fellowmen as our God wants it.*
>
> *Eric, as you found your God in America, so I found Him during the first world war. I thank Him daily for all the good He has done to us.*

As the years hasten past, "swifter than a weaver's shuttle," Eric knows that the truth he grasped so many years ago will hold him fast by God's mighty power even unto the end.

The carefree child-
hood days in Unsen.
Here Eric and Irmgard
posed for a snapshot
in the flower garden
behind the *Gasthaus*.

When Father visited
home, on furlough, the
Kreye family posed for
a portrait. Eric is at
left.

The Gasthaus

The Gasthaus and attached farm buildings.

Eric and his parents, Wilhelm and Johanna Kreye.

Backyard with favorite pear tree.

The *Süntelturm,* some distance from the small village of Unsen, was always an intriguing spot for Eric and his two friends. From its serrated top one can see many miles in every direction.

The schoolchildren from Unsen enjoyed the walk to Holtensen, especially in the spring when the apple trees were in full blossom.

This picture, taken very recently, shows the old school in Holtensen. It was here where Herr Meier jumped from desk to desk in madness, and where later many of the Hitler Youth activities took place.

A corner of the *Gastzimmer* (guest room) where
Eric helped serve beer and other drinks. Here Father
entertained guests, some being high-ranking Nazi
officials.

This huge barn door, now wide open, was often closed during the war years—for many a secret was hidden behind it.

It was a good thing that the secret police never looked under the piles of firewood!

The Thorvaldsson family, Johann, David, Danny, Eric's sister Irmgard, and Arni.

Eric, his wife Arbie, and daughters Linda and Nancy.